Praise for *Why Smart Women Make Bad Decisions*

'The thing about Annie McCubbin's writing is the detail. It's specific and concrete and it makes you laugh out loud when you read it because you instantly relate to it. It's great storytelling, and because the story in this book is so good, you remember the science that goes with it.'

Katrina Foster, Lecturer, Writing for Performance, UTS

'Wow! What an achievement. I loved every part of it and wished it wouldn't end.'

Nikki Pender, NZ barrister and business director

'A book for our times – a serious yet entertaining look at how women can take control personally and professionally. It is also a book for men, who will surely recognise themselves or their friends somewhere in these pages and be motivated to act.'

Dagmar Schmidmaier AM, Director, CEW Leaders Program

'Engaging, humorous and thought-provoking, *Why Smart Women Make Bad Decisions* is a must-read for every 25- to 45-year-old woman.'

Amelia Russell, retail buying manager

'Kat's fast-moving second-person inner-monologue made me laugh out loud! Her skewed observations and tangled rationalisations are relatable to many experiences I would rather not admit having. Annie McCubbin uses her humour and humanity to share some pertinent insights into how we can untangle our thinking and engage more meaningfully with ourselves and those around us.'

Odile LeClezio, actor and voice coach

'Loved it. Funny and informative. It's a great read on, let's face it, what could be a very dry topic.'

Vicki Yep, nursing unit manager

'This is brilliant. The book that HAS to be read right now. My genuine hope is that this book is lapped up.'

Lyndall Russell, clinical psychotherapist and transformational leadership strategist

WHY SMART WOMEN
MAKE BAD DECISIONS

Why smart women make bad decisions

and how critical thinking can protect them

Annie McCubbin

For David, Lily and Lachlan.
Thank you for pretending not to notice
when I feed the dog at the table.

Also by Annie McCubbin: *Why Smart Women Buy the Lies and How Critical Thinking Reveals the Truth*

First published in 2021 by Major Street Publishing Pty Ltd. Reprinted in 2022 and 2023.
E: info@majorstreet.com.au W: majorstreet.com.au M | +61 421 707 983

A catalogue record for this book is available from the National Library of Australia

Printed book ISBN: 978-0-6489804-4-5
Ebook ISBN: 978-0-6489804-5-2

Cover design by Tess McCabe
Internal design by Production Works
Printed in Australia by IVE.

10 9 8 7 6 5 4 3

Disclaimer: The material in this publication is in the nature of general comment only, and neither purports nor intends to be advice. Readers should not act on the basis of any matter in this publication without considering (and if appropriate taking) professional advice with due regard to their own particular circumstances. The author and publisher expressly disclaim all and any liability to any person, whether a purchaser of this publication or not, in respect of anything and the consequences of anything done or omitted to be done by any such person in reliance, whether whole or partial, upon the whole or any part of the contents of this publication.

Contents

'The default mode of human psychology is to grab onto comforting beliefs for purely emotional reasons, and then justify those beliefs to ourselves...'

Dr Steven Novella, MD, clinical neurologist and host of *The Skeptics Guide to the Universe*

Preface

Imagine this.

A picture of a woman – slim, hair pulled back into a ponytail, no makeup, perfect skin. She's standing triumphantly on top of a mountain looking out over a vast vista. There is mist in the valleys; it could even be sunrise. At her feet is a backpack. The implication is she rose early, climbed alone, and she's savouring the rich reward of her efforts.

The caption underneath the picture says something like:

Live your best life.

This statement is worthy and appealing but it's also general and vague. I'd really like to be living my best life, you might think, but what does it look like and why aren't I currently doing it?

What the caption should say is:

Identify the cognitive flaws in your thinking and improve the quality of your life across all contexts.

The fact is, a lack of critical-thinking skills contributes mightily to the problems in our lives, but introducing the notion of *meta-cognition* and advising people to *think about their thinking* is a difficult message to sell. It's not full of easy promise. So, we listen to advice that *is* full of promise, and often offers magical solutions to our knotty life problems. The major thrust of this advice encourages people everywhere to trust their gut, to sit in the stillness and wait for the voice of truth to arise from deep within.

The Universe will lead you. Think positively. Magic will happen if you let it.

Now let me state right upfront: I know our gut and intuition are amazing. I'm all for allowing our intuition to guide us. Just not in all contexts.

Our intuition is fabulous. It is responsible for our creativity. It is our protector in a dark car park late at night when it tells us there's danger afoot. Intuition saves us time, cutting through unnecessary analysis to arrive at brilliant decisions. It makes us perceptive, quick and decisive.

But because our intuition can be so right, it's easy to assume it is right all the time.

It is not.

The truth is, our intuition, like all our mental and emotional functions, is limited, often flawed, and quite often highly inaccurate.

The key to getting our lives back on track is understanding how deeply irrational and flawed our brains are.

Now, there's no shortage of books and podcasts selling the message 'Let your Gut be your Guide'. And, if you look for them, there are plenty of critical-thinking books as well – but their message is not as sexy. They're certainly no match for the writings of 'Warrior Women' and 'Guru Guy', so their message is lost.

When we're choosing the coat, the restaurant, the gym, the dog (a Groodle in case you're wondering), the career move or the partner, the stakes are high. Yet our analysis of the thinking that goes into these decisions is low.

When we're making a decision, our thought process should be something like: 'I have a strong feeling in my gut about this, but should I be trusting it?'

There is a lot of good science out there. It can be utilised to work out when your brain can be trusted and when it's feeding you fake news. But we are more inclined to be attracted to the notion that there is meaning in the things that happen to us, and that our intuition is leading us down the right path.

Challenging some of these deeply held beliefs can make us extremely uncomfortable. Considered analysis just isn't as seductive as the spiritual slogan. This is why so many well-educated, intelligent people are wooed by simplistic and romantic assertions.

The absence of critical thinking is understandable. Being understandable, though, doesn't make it right.

So, I have written a book about how the flaws in your thinking can make you susceptible to poor decision-making and exploitation. We follow the life of Kat, a thirty-something woman who, while in the midst of a fractious breakup, still has to deal with the everyday challenges of being a working woman. She pitches an idea to the insurance firm she works for, endures a performance review, has a breakdown in front of her neighbours, learns Morse code, goes to a party, stalks her ex on Facebook, goes away for a weekend and, as the story progresses, begins to understand some of the flaws in her thinking.

Every chapter of the story is followed by an analysis of the cognitive biases that shaped her decision-making.

Women are particularly vulnerable to the 'trust your gut' message. Women are particularly vulnerable to being gaslighted. Consider your own experience and the experiences of your friends and family members. How many decisions have been made off the back of 'a feeling'? How have they worked out? I imagine brilliantly sometimes, and other times disastrously. How did you talk about it afterwards? Did you get closer to the truth?

Wouldn't you like to understand the pitfalls in your thinking so you can steer your life with a steadier hand?

Then read on.

1

Kat and The Hipster

For the first time since the breakup, you do not have to sprint for the bus. You are leaving the flat on time. You have managed to put a load out and feed the cat. Your handbag is over your shoulder, your KeepCup is in your hand, and you are about to pull the front door shut, when a retching sound stops you in your tracks.

You pause, your hand on the doorknob.

Then, your brain catches up, and notifies you that the sound is not a good one. You throw yourself into reverse, fling the door back open, and lurch back into the flat.

The Cat is vomiting in the lounge room.

You reach for The Cat, trip on the rug, and your KeepCup shatters.

You rise from the floor, dust the glass shards from the knees of your new linen pants, and stand gaping at the defiled floor.

You curse The Cat.

She is now sitting on the kitchen bench, looking at you implacably. She seems to have recovered.

You find it viciously unfair that the KeepCup has dropped on the unforgiving surface of the floorboards, while The Cat has elected to vomit on the absorbent nap of the rug.

The rug was new and The Cat's interest in its arrival only seemed piqued when the opportunity to vomit on it was presented.

After the gag-inducing clean up, you are now Late. You sprint for the bus, miss it by ten seconds, have to get an Uber and abstain from your morning coffee, as you can't bear the disapproving face of Dean, the vegan activist barista, without your KeepCup.

As you arrive at the office you comfort yourself that Bad Things Always Happen in Threes, and you've had your quota for the day.

Though, thinking about it, there have actually been four, if you count the Missed Coffee on top of the Broken KeepCup.

Actually, five, if you count the Uber in a separate category to the Missed Bus.

This is a worrying thought. It means you could now be in the second tranche of Bad Things Happening in Threes, which means you're waiting for the Sixth Bad Thing.

Christine appears at your desk to present you with the Sixth Bad Thing.

She tells you that you sent version 2.3, instead of 2.4, to the Head of HR. You smile apologetically at Christine, while you fire up your computer. You find twenty-five emails telling you the same thing.

'They're waiting in the meeting room to talk about version control,' says Christine.

You pick up your staff room coffee cup, which says *Go For It, Legend*, when your phone buzzes.

Your heart leaps.

It's The Hipster.

You scroll down the text looking for the words, 'I'm sorry.'

They're not there.

He's texting to say his friend Anton is coming tonight to pick up the couch.

You wish you had version control over The Hipster. You'd go with an earlier one.

'It's not convenient,' you text back. 'I'm out.'

'No problem,' texts The Hipster. 'I've given him my key.'

You start writing 'Give me back my key,' then delete it. Maybe having the key means he's still thinking of coming back.

Your phone buzzes again. It's your sister, Samantha. The text reads, 'Toby just proposed. Am sobbing. With Joy of Course. Head bridesmaid, darling. As discussed, caramel.' You'll look hideous in caramel. Samantha has been planning her wedding since she was four, so she'll probably have it ready to go in three months. That gives you under three months to lose the 2.75 kilos. You're regretting the cinnamon scroll you scoffed this morning in place of the Missed Coffee.

You realise Christine is speaking to you again.

'Yes,' you say, 'I'm coming.'

Before you can rise from your seat your star performer, Jay, comes over, threatening to quit. This is the Seventh Bad Thing today. This could be the beginning of the third tranche of Bad Things. He tells you he can no longer tolerate working with Lisa (pronounced Liza).

'Yes,' you say to Jay, 'I completely understand. Leave it with me.'

You can't tolerate working with Lisa (pronounced Liza) either. The problem is you're her boss, yet you find her a bit scary.

'That's what you said last week,' he says.

'Yes, I know. I've been snowed under.'

You're flat-chat busy. You don't have the time to have endless Performance Management conversations every time there's a problem in the team. Also, you'd attempted to have a Performance Management conversation with Lisa last Wednesday, which ended in you implying she was in line for a promotion, so what's the point?

'Also,' Jay says, 'What's happened to your hair?

'I have alopecia,' you say. 'It's genetic.'

This is not true. You've been so stressed that you've literally been pulling your hair out. You're beginning to suspect that this run of bad luck is karma for the amount of mean, vengeful things you've been thinking and for putting your wine bottles in Mrs Hume's bin.

Anyway, Lisa (pronounced Liza) led you astray at her interview. She was impressive, articulate and funny.

She's not funny now.

Since her arrival a month ago, your previously harmonious workgroup has splintered into multiple warring factions. Lisa either inspires great loyalty or committed loathing. She's aggressive, defensive and petty. Not to mention lazy, divisive and belligerent.

She's eaten your lunch from the mini fridge. Twice. She flatly denied it while wiping the telltale haloumi crumbs from her mouth. She could stare down Putin if required.

Her red hair – which she is not pulling out strand by strand – serves as a trigger for anxiety every time you pass her desk. Maybe, like Donald Trump, she will rise to great heights. She could take your job, then end up running the entire organisation on the back of her schismatic personality, lack of expertise in any area and breathtaking self-belief.

Your phone beeps again. It's someone called Meredith texting about the room to rent. You dislike her use of smiling emojis and text her back saying it's taken. You just can't interview another potential flatmate. After hiring Lisa (pronounced Liza), your confidence in your interviewing ability has plummeted.

'Are you alright?' asks Jay.

'Yes,' you say. You look at your hand. You've pulled out another four hairs. That's okay, only 109,459 to go before you'll need a wig.

Exactly four weeks ago, there was no Lisa (pronounced Liza), no cat vomit, no version-control problem, no broken KeepCup, no broken heart, no trichotillomania and your hair was still your most impressive feature. On the same morning you interviewed Lisa, you woke at 6.30 to find The Cat sitting on The Hipster's warm pillow, regarding you genially. The Hipster's bearded head normally remained in residence on the pillow long after you'd risen. You'd become adept at avoiding the three recalcitrant floorboards, as he was prone to developing migraines if woken by floor-generated noises.

The day before, however, The Hipster had cleaned furiously in preparation for the upcoming real estate inspection, and that day he had risen early to bring you a cup of tea in bed. With normal milk. He only drank almond milk, as products produced from a cow offended him. However, that morning he'd overcome his distaste and smiled as he handed you the cup.

You'd had a strong feeling this relationship was *meant to be* the first time you looked into his eyes. 'We will grow old together,' he'd said the night you'd met. He moved into your flat a month later.

Accepting the cup of tea, you recalled the real estate agent, Rebecca, saying how beautifully you kept your flat, and what a lovely man your partner was.

You drained your cup and lay on your side looking at him across the room, doing an efficient downward-facing dog in the slanting sunlight. It's true, you thought. He is lovely. He stretched luxuriously, took your empty cup from you, ran his fingers through your hair and strolled towards the kitchen – perhaps, you thought wondrously, to unpack the dishwasher. It seemed anything was possible that morning.

The Hipster had been encouraging you to do a gratitude meditation every day, saying it opened channels to receiving all the things you deserved from the Universe. You'd been applying yourself assiduously to the task, sitting compliantly with The Hipster on the floor on a special Gratitude Meditation Cushion. Apparently, the cushion was important: it helped with alignment of the spine. You were unsure why spinal alignment was important.

Early on you'd asked The Hipster, 'But what if somebody disabled meditates, and they can't sit on a cushion or keep their spine straight?'

'Kitten,' The Hipster had said, stroking the inside of your wrist, 'how about you just try and quiet down that brain of yours and sit in some stillness for a bit?' The Hipster's beard gave him a Jesus look, which you knew wasn't congruent with meditation and veganism, but nevertheless, you found it reassuring.

Admittedly, during each meditation you struggled not to think about how many calories you'd consumed that day, juxtaposed against the amount of exercise you'd done.

Still, The Hipster delivering your tea that morning was so close to your vision of him being the domestically vigilant, sexy, affectionate partner you'd always dreamt of, that you felt yourself to be a sorceress of Universal Magic.

Or was it sorcerer? Perhaps sorceress was redundant, like 'actress'. It might be a mistake to use gender-specific terminology in the Universal realm.

You leant back on the pillows and ran your own fingers through your hair, which, unassailed by humidity, was organised attractively on the pillow. You wished The Hipster would return to see you displayed so enticingly, but you comforted yourself with the thought that his absence may indicate domestic engagement. Seconds later you heard the first affirming noise of a glass being returned to the cupboard. Your life was complete.

Tidy flat.

The Hipster attentive, with increasing levels of domestic awareness.

Hair fantastic.

Three Good Things in a row. It was definitely going to be a good day. Even the normally disdainful Cat was positively collegial. You were so awash with love that, for minutes at a time, you forgot to worry about your recent 2.75-kilogram weight gain.

Later, as you left the flat, you noted your lovely man partner had put the recycle bin out, unasked. You nodded at Mrs Hume from Flat Ten, who was tersely rearranging all the bins centimetre by centimetre. All except yours. The look of your bin already sitting perfectly aligned on the verge filled you with joy.

Your bus pulled into the stop the exact moment you arrived, and your favourite seat was loyally waiting for you. At work you swept into the waiting lift like royalty, and Madelaine, from the eleventh floor, who habitually speaks loudly to you while staring at your forehead, was nowhere in sight.

That was the second tranche of Three Good Things. You were on fire.

At morning tea, though not a gambler, you bought a scratchie and scored an instant $50. Such was your confidence in being 'in flow' with the Universe, you gave the $50 to a homeless man and his adorable Border Collie.

Your phone buzzed with a text. It was The Hipster. A trail of heart emojis followed his proclamation of love. You stood in the street smiling stupidly at your phone.

You were unstoppable. The stars were aligned. The Universe had your back. You were actually looking forward to conducting the interviews for a new team member. You just knew the perfect candidate was going to show up. You could feel it in your bones. And like magic, there she was: Lisa (pronounced Liza) Miles, the first candidate.

You'd known it instinctively as soon as she'd walked in the door with her uniform fake tan. Her attention to detail around the problem areas of wrist and elbow was exemplary. Admittedly she was late, but a flat tyre could happen to anyone, and the way she told the story was so engaging, you were immediately impressed with her communication skills. She was smart, too; smarter in fact than her CV suggested, and though she'd held a lot of different positions over the last three years, she'd explained that sometimes her capacity to think outside the box was not welcomed.

Well, thinking outside the box was exactly what you were after. You liked her. She was responsive, considered in her answers and funny. She was your girl and she was going to be the perfect team member.

STOP TRUSTING YOUR INSTINCTS – SOME OF THEM ARE RUBBISH

Okay. Welcome to Kat's life, where things aren't going too well. Kat is smart, but her thinking, like yours and mine, is flawed, and those flaws influence her decision-making. Decisions she made on the day when she was feeling positive are still influencing her life a month later, and not in a good way.

There are some cognitive traps that will become evident as we watch Kat navigate her way through life. So, what can we learn from her experiences? What can we do to make sure we don't fall into the same potholes? Well, let's start with what *not* to do.

Your intuition is tricky

Don't indiscriminately trust your intuitive voice. That's the first cab off the rank. Why? Because traps in your thinking arise out of your intuitive responses.

'Leave my intuition alone,' I hear you say. 'My intuition is incredibly accurate. It's saved me from bad situations so many times.'

I'm sure it has! But, if you analyse your life through a certain lens, you'll find that sometimes your intuition has been right, and sometimes it's been wrong. However, because of one of our brain bugs called *confirmation bias*, you only remember the hits and not the misses. Confirmation bias is just one of many brain glitches that, if not recognised and attended to, can send your life careering in an unwanted direction.

So, what exactly is intuition? Well, it's when you just *know* things. Our intuition is our ability to reach a quick and ready judgement about something without going through a rational analytical process.

Our intuition can tell us things like: 'I really like this person I'm interviewing,' or 'This guy is really nice,' or 'This diet I've just read about on my smartphone looks really good,' or 'Don't go to the gym tonight, you've had a rough day, exercise some self-care, stay home and have a nice glass of pinot.'

We call it our 'gut feeling'. It feels good to go with your gut. It feels right. Our bookshelves, TVs and podcasts are awash with information pointing to the conclusion that your intuition is a hallowed instrument of truth.

In fact, intuition is very likely *causing* problems in your life. Your thinking is littered with cognitive biases leading you down the wrong path, again and again. These cognitive biases are sneaky and deserve your attention.

In the story, cognitive bias led Kat to believe she was making rational decisions. She felt strongly that Lisa was the right candidate, that The Hipster was the right partner and that her day was going well. Feelings are important, and nobody should ever tell you your feelings are wrong. But feeling something 'very strongly' doesn't mean you have to act on it. It just means you have a strong feeling.

Indeed, one of the core themes of Kat's story is that intuition is susceptible to error and manipulation and it should not be accepted uncritically.

The false god of the New Age

One of the places these cognitive biases do their sneaking around is in the sentiments of a lot of New-Age thinking. We are told to tune into our deep, intuitive voice; that success lies in our connection to our higher selves.

And where do these messages from our higher selves come from?

Our brains.

The bit that's left out of this highly appealing narrative is how flawed it is. Our feelings should, of course, always be acknowledged. Always. But are they necessarily the harbingers of truth?

Introducing your limbic system

The brain is extremely complex, but for the purposes of understanding where decisions are made in our brain, we are going to basically look at two of its parts. One is the limbic system: the emotional seat of our brain. The other part is our frontal lobe: the rational, reasoning part of the brain, where planning and executive function occur.

So, if we go back to Kat's story where her day was *not* going well, her limbic system – the emotional part of her brain – was telling her to avoid having a difficult conversation with Lisa, as she felt intimidated. This was all subconscious. Kat was aware she found Lisa scary, but not so much that it was going to affect her decision-making. The next part of the process was also subconscious for Kat, and she was unaware of it happening. Her frontal lobe – the rational, planning, decision-making, social moderating part of her brain – post-rationalised her feelings of being intimidated and came up with an explanation that made Kat feel okay about herself: that she was busy, and it was pointless talking to Lisa anyway.

The limbic system makes decisions for us, unbeknown to our conscious brain, and the frontal lobe is left trying to post-rationalise that decision. This process goes on day-in, day-out, because the limbic system (where intuition springs from) is vital for our survival. We need subconscious processing to function in our everyday lives. We don't have the mental bandwidth to consciously examine every bit of information taken in by our senses. The subconscious part of our brain takes in vast amounts of data all the time. Think of your subconscious as a massive supercomputer, and the conscious part of your brain like an early edition smartphone. Our conscious brains are just no match for our subconscious brains in terms of speed and data storage. We are only consciously aware of a tiny portion of that data at any time.

A good moment to listen to your gut

You are in a dark car park late at night and feel an intuitive sense of danger. Acting on that gut instinct could save your life. Your subconscious has scanned the environment and told you to get in your car quickly and drive away. Do not hesitate. Do what it's urging you to do. Your subconscious is picking up data from the environment and giving you signals. Get in the car, lock the door and drive.

This more primitive part of your brain developed millions of years ago, before we had language, when we were roaming around on the savannah. (Not carrying designer handbags, just to clarify.) It developed to deal with a much simpler and more dangerous world, when the possibility of being some lion's dinner was still on the cards – and not because you'd jumped out of the four-wheel drive to retrieve your phone while on safari at Kruger.

Our brains were designed for a more dangerous time and are easily spooked.

With an ancient computer in her head, Kat didn't know the difference between an aggressive person in her team and being confronted by a lion at the mouth of her cave. It's why holding her ground with Lisa felt so dangerous.

We too can feel like we're making rational choices when we're actually being guided by the flawed calculations of our primitive brain. So, as we follow Kat and observe her dealing with challenges common to most of us, the tricky role of the subconscious will become more and more evident – as will the errors in our processing and the flaws in our thinking. We'll see how these errors affect her decision-making, and the impact that has on different areas of her life. If Kat can learn to identify the bugs and flaws in her brain and understand how powerful her subconscious is, she can learn to live in a less reactive way.

This is not a book about creative visualisation

Author's note: when I say 'the subconscious parts of our brain are powerful', I'm not saying you can harness the subconscious to manifest whatever you like. It's not that kind of story.

But this is a better story. It's more productive to identify the bugs in your thinking that contribute to you making rubbish decisions, than hope the universe will intervene and grant your deepest desire. The idea of 'manifesting' also gives us a false sense of control over our lives, allowing us to cling to the hope that thinking or meditating on what we want will magically make it appear. You're better off spending your time doing practical things in the real world.

Critical-thinking skills are the bomb

Think of yourself as an actor on stage, with your life as the performance. You feel like you're in control of your performance: that every action is your choice. But in reality, it's more like you're a marionette – while you're standing on stage performing your current scene, your cognitive biases are on a platform above the stage in the darkness, pulling your strings. So practiced and deft are they at the string pulling, you're not even aware they're there. So instead of your character reaching for the chamomile tea, she mixes a margarita. You look at your hand and think to yourself, 'This was an alcohol-free night. Oh well, now I've made it, shame for it to go to waste!'

But all is not lost. You are not destined to forever be helpless in the face of unseen machinations. By the time you've finished reading Kat's story, you should be able to pause the performance of your own life, ask the audience to wait a minute, shine the torch your character is holding up into the darkness, and tell those sub-conscious processes you know *exactly* what they're doing. You can demand they cut the strings. Be firm with them. You're running the show now. That's how you mitigate their influence: you use your new-found understanding to illuminate their role in your performance. Then you're free to think analytically and rationally about why you're doing what you're doing, and thinking what you're thinking.

Introducing patternicity

Okay, come on, 'fess up. Do you think bad things happen in threes? You're not alone.

But do they?

Well, probably not.

Kat, like the rest of us, saw patterns in the development of her days. When things were going badly, she saw the negative events in her day as happening in lots of three. Once the cat vomited on her new rug, her KeepCup broke and she missed the bus, she felt confident there would be no more bad things in that day, as she had completed the magic three. But then she realised a fourth bad thing had happened (the missed coffee), so she had to start counting another three, and then another.

It was the same with the good day. The idea that there was already a pattern of good things happening in threes predisposed her to think the afternoon's interview with Lisa Miles was going to go well.

Humans love looking for patterns. We love it so much we do it subconsciously, and when we think we detect one, we invest it with meaning.

'Patternicity', a term coined by science writer Michael Shermer, is the tendency to find meaningful patterns in meaningless noise – hence, two bad things happen then you wait for the third. It gives a sense of order to chaos. It is a cognitive bias left over from a period when identifying patterns was essential for our survival. For example, when wandering about on the savannah, it was good practice to notice paw prints in the sand, in case it meant a lion was near. It was also good to track the pattern of seasons, as that was essential for survival.

Unfortunately, however, we also notice patterns when they're not really there.

Introducing magical thinking

Magical thinking is everywhere and wears a lot of different guises. One guise suggests that if you wish really hard (often dressed up as a meditative practice) you can change your fortunes. Another guise suggests that if you have a lot of negative thoughts, you could in turn create negative events in your life.

Kat believed the gratitude meditation encouraged by The Hipster produced the positive events in her life, and that the negative events were tit-for-tat karma at play. Since the interview with Lisa came after a series of positive events in the day, Lisa was placed into the 'Going Well' bucket. Therefore, her positive characteristics were painted in bright, bold colours, and anything negative was quickly dismissed.

Author's note: the universe is a big thing with stars and planets. It doesn't care about you. It's not involved in the day-to-day workings of your life, and it is not planning life lessons for you.

Yes, what you think influences your behaviour, but your thoughts don't have a special energetic influence of their own. One of the worst sorts of magical thinking is believing that all illness is the result of negative thinking, negative belief systems or karma. To suggest people are responsible for 'creating their illness' via their thinking is pernicious, simplistic and dangerous.

It's just magical thinking. All of it. And belief in magical thinking can be bolstered by patternicity – the thinker sees a pattern between their internal thinking and the world around them.

Was it really 'meant to be'?

'Bad things happen in threes' lies in the same realm as saying it was 'meant to be' when something good or bad happens. Kat felt very strongly that her relationship was meant to be.

Was it? Why?

People often use the phrase 'It was meant to be' when something is going well. It could be a big thing, like finding your life partner, or a small thing, like finding the perfect car park. The phrase also gets an outing when someone has a painful breakup or experiences some other distressing event. If you extrapolate that thought out, then you'd have to believe that *everything* happens because it was meant to be. So, is it meant to be when a mother in a refugee camp loses her child to dysentery? When a lonely seventy-year-old man loses his entire life savings to a romance scam? Are we saying that all negative events happen for a reason? Seems a bit brutal. Perhaps this magical, mysterious energy that apparently finds people convenient car parks and perfect partners could be co-opted to sort childhood poverty.

Just a thought.

It's comforting to think that things happen for a reason. No-one likes to be rejected. Our thinking is littered with aphorisms like 'One door shuts and another one opens' – sayings that we've adopted because they give us a reassuring sense that there's meaning behind our lives. They make life seem less chaotic.

So, what's the problem with that? What's wrong with believing bad things happen in threes, or that you're on a roll so it's a good day to buy a lottery ticket? Where's the harm in believing such things? Well, if we believe there's meaning in the random things that happen in our lives, then we may develop a tendency to look for meaning in situations and come up with the wrong answer – which could lead to poor decision-making.

For example, let's say you're in a relationship that is unsatisfying. You might think to yourself, 'Well, this relationship isn't great, but maybe I'm meant to be in it. Maybe it's teaching me something. Maybe I'm meant to stay.' This sort of thinking, where you're ascribing a higher purpose to your situation, muddies the water for more clarifying critical thinking. If you remove the notion that things happen for a reason, you can look at the situation, whatever it is, with clear eyes. If you're more in control of your thinking in this way, you can have an incredibly meaningful life without magical thinking cluttering it up.

Luck has gone out of fashion – let's bring it back!

Realistically, how well your day – or, in fact, your life – goes is a combination of a whole lot of things, with some luck thrown in. Luck seems to have gone out of fashion. Of course, how hard you work, your attitude and the socioeconomics you were born into all have a huge influence on the fortunes in your life. But luck has a big part, too. The co-occurrence of so many positive things in Kat's happy morning was just coincidence, as were the negative things that transpired on the day that began with the cat vomiting. There was no underlying meaning to the morning's events, but Kat ascribed meaning to them. Then, once she'd layered on some magical thinking, she was primed to make some poor decisions.

We're influenced by our moods, and often not in a good way

During her happy day, Kat felt great. What's wrong with that? It's better than being in a rubbish mood. Studies have found that our thinking and decision-making are affected by our moods, good or bad. Happy people are more likely to anticipate that a picnic will have nice weather than sad people. People in a good mood tend to think that those around them are more skilled than those in a bad mood. People in a bad mood are more likely to attribute negative intent to another person. This can flow on to affect our behaviour.

By the time Kat was on her way to work on her positive day, she already had patternicity in her corner, telling her this was a good day so things were going to continue to be good. She had magical thinking adding an extra layer of legitimacy to this thought, by implying her happy morning was the product of her own enlightened internal reality. She was in a good mood when Lisa walked in the door – her gut told her that Lisa was the perfect candidate. It felt right; Kat could feel it in her bones.

But Kat's gut was wrong. Intuition, patternicity and luck came together to create a fallacious sense of certainty, coaxing her into making a bad decision with ongoing ramifications.

Liking or disliking someone on sight should not be the final word on them.

Beware your happy mood doesn't lead you to:

- Sign up for six months of hot yoga sessions.
- Agree to attend a Scientology session when approached on a street corner by a guy with a personality test.
- Hire someone because your subconscious gave you the nod.
- Eat a Krispy Kreme.
- Like someone on sight.

Beware of liking someone, or feeling overly positive about someone, on sight. Case in point: Kat liked Lisa on sight. Part of the appeal was that Lisa was very charming; but charming doesn't necessarily mean good, and lack of charm doesn't mean bad. Apparently, Kim Jong-un is a complete sweetie when you meet him, and many brilliant doctors have the personalities of mullets.

Now, as we have discussed, sometimes your intuition might be accurate. You might have developed a precise antenna for certain behavioural tendencies. For instance, perhaps you are attuned to the feeling of being manipulated. In this case, your gut response to the notion of being manipulated should be factored into your analysis; but it shouldn't be the end of the story.

Beware your unhappy mood doesn't lead you to:

- Sign up for six months of hot yoga sessions.

- Agree to attend a Scientology session when approached on a street corner by a guy with a personality test.

- Hire someone because your subconscious gave you the nod.

- Eat a number of Krispy Kremes.

- Dislike someone on sight.

Often, disliking someone on sight is your subconscious working behind the scenes, digging around in your old files and finding similar features. A perfectly nice man might share the handlebar moustache of a loathed teacher, triggering a response.

When Kat's day was hijacked by the vomiting cat, the sense of doom that she was in for a bad day affected her thinking and sent her into spiralling anxiety. She couldn't face the barista without her cup, she dreaded the meeting about version control and, more importantly, she couldn't deal with the issue of Lisa, who was causing a lot of trouble in her team.

Confirmation bias – the mother of all biases

Confirmation bias is our tendency to cherrypick available information to confirm what we already think. It's when we interpret and remember things in ways that validate our existing position. We all do it, all the time.

Scenario A: your partner leaves wet towels on the bed.

You've had a heated exchange about your partner not being a child, and you not being the parent. A month later, you notice the offending towels are still *always* being left on the bed, whereas your partner swears he or she *always* hangs them up now. Who's right?

Well, you're both right. You're both being cognitively hijacked by confirmation bias. You *only* notice when your partner leaves the towels on the bed, and he or she *only* notices when the towels are hung up. Mystery solved!

Scenario B: you read a report that chocolate is a most excellent food for your health and should be consumed daily.

You also read a report that chocolate is the most appalling food of all time and you shouldn't touch it. You only remember the first report, which confirms the positive qualities of chocolate, because you love it and can't imagine life without it.

Confirmation bias led Kat to only focus on the things about Lisa that confirmed her belief that Lisa was the best candidate. She admired her uniformly applied fake tan; she found her positive and charming; she excused her lateness; she rationalised away her lack of previous job stability. In other words, she interpreted the situation and evidence in front of her in a way that supported her initial position via her gut instinct: that Lisa was 'the one'.

The notion that good or bad things happen in threes is classic confirmation bias. When you expect things to happen in threes, you're on the lookout for it and select situations in your environment to confirm your belief.

Primacy and recency effects (watch out for them in restaurants)

The primacy effect is a cognitive bias causing us to remember the information presented first. A typical example of when you might fall victim to the primacy effect is when you go to a restaurant and choose a dish near the beginning of the menu. Restaurants often take advantage of this brain bias and put their most profitable item at the top of the menu – perhaps even at the top right-hand side, where our eyes go first. Sneaky!

The recency effect means we are also more likely to remember information presented last. If we are presented with a long list of words and asked to recall them later, we will remember the words at the beginning of the list (primacy effect) or at the end of the list (recency effect) with greater speed and accuracy than those in the middle.

The same can apply to a schedule of candidates. Due to these biases, the first and last candidates interviewed are more likely to stick in the interviewers' minds, giving them an edge. On top of everything else, Kat fell victim to the primacy effect: Lisa was the first candidate interviewed, and was therefore subconsciously favoured.

Getting smarter

Kat is not stupid. Kat is, in fact, very clever. However, being influenced by these brain glitches is not ameliorated by being smart. Glitches in Kat's cognition were able to cloud her mind and guide her decision-making, and this is the danger. These cognitive pitfalls are not harmless: they are wildly influential in the course of our lives. Our brains – our own minds – can work against our best interests and leave us with misplaced confidence and understanding, and faulty impressions of the world.

Kat felt that charismatic, red-haired, first-in-the-door Lisa Miles was right for the job. If she'd slowed down and thought about it – taken heed of the warning signs and been a little more analytical and measured – things might have gone differently. But she *felt* that Lisa was right. She just *knew*. All these brain glitches worked together to create a strong feeling of certainty, and Kat took it at face value. And she paid dearly for that choice.

This is why it is worthwhile to pick apart these error tendencies in our neural machines. Stuff happens. We can only control our circumstances to a certain extent. But by understanding the biases, the flaws in our brains, we can try to mitigate their sway over our mental processing. We can have better control of how we think, and how that affects our decision-making. There is no magical trick – no silver bullet – but knowing some of the brain bugs causing havoc with your thinking is a good start.

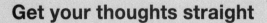

Get your thoughts straight

The Gambler's Mistake

Notice whether you're seeing patterns where they actually don't exist, except in your imagination – for example, do you think you're having a run of good or bad luck?

The Happiness Error

Make a note of the differences in your decision-making when you're in a good mood or a bad mood.

You're Not a Magician

Watch for instances where you've layered meaning onto a situation – for example, you visualised a car park and found one, or you were thinking about someone and they called.

Escape the Bubble

Watch out for only registering information that you already agree with. Take a note of how your social media reflects back what you already believe.

Seek Out the Devil

Make a point of seeking an opinion that is antithetical to the one you hold.

Left or Right

Watch when you look at a menu. See if your eyes go to the top right-hand corner of the page first.

2

Kat is single

You're finally home after sitting in filthy traffic for seventy minutes, due to a road upgrade you'd feebly protested against. You spent the entire journey seething with resentment because the idea you expressed in March, which was summarily dismissed, was today regurgitated by Liam from Finance, and greeted with table-thumping enthusiasm.

You dump your keys on the hall table and come face-to-face with The Hipster's Deepak Chopra poster.

Gratitude opens the door to the Power, the Wisdom,
the Creativity of the Universe.

You're experiencing difficulty finding your Gratitude right now. You're grumpy, tired, want a drink, and someone finished the bottle of wine from last night. You gave up on Dry July, Dry February and Dry May, and your two alcohol-free nights a week have diminished to one a month.

You spend a good five minutes rifling through the pantry looking for the ancient bottle of sherry and railing about the finished wine before you remember it was you who finished it. This shouldn't have been a difficult conclusion to reach. You live alone.

So, you're standing in front of the fridge with your handbag still over your shoulder, scrounging for food. You find an old rind of cheddar and some five-day-old rocket. You contemplate making a salade niçoise but you're missing tomatoes, tuna, eggs, olives and anchovies.

You open a can of chickpeas. You're pretty sure they're a superfood. You can have them with the sliver of cheddar. You go to the bedroom, where you divest yourself of your handbag, and return to find The Cat on the counter insouciantly eating the rind.

She's not even your cat. She's The Hipster's cat, which he took when he left six weeks ago, but in some feat of cat echolocation and endurance she has returned to you. You'd come home to find her sitting on the window ledge outside, one paw on the glass.

'What?' you'd said. 'What? You don't live here anymore. Go home.'

She had sat there for six hours. Staring at you. Not even meowing. You'd found her imperious as opposed to plaintive, which irritated you. You'd tapped on the glass and made shooing noises. You'd drunk a glass of wine in front of her while asking her if she knew why The Hipster had left. You'd briefly wept while pressing your hand up to the window near her paw. You'd told her you recently developed an allergy to cats. She was impervious. You'd contemplated returning her, but this would require making a phone call to The Hipster during which you suspected you'd come across more Pauline Hanson than Jennifer Lawrence.

Finally, you'd found the disloyalty of The Cat satisfying. You'd opened the window.

You tip the can of chickpeas onto a plate you've dug out of the dirty dishes in the sink and sit on the couch. The Cat looks at you.

'You're eating the cheese,' you say. 'Leave me to my chickpeas.'

The Cat meows.

This triggers a desperate desire to hear The Hipster's voice. You open Facebook to distract yourself. The first post you see features the inspirational words of Thobra Khan, splayed over an unlikely sunlit field of lavender, stating that:

What you Resist in your partner is a reflection of yourself.
Do not Resist. There are No Accidents. No Happenstance.
Accept what the Universe has planned for you and
Seek the Lesson.

You are irritated by the Capricious use of capital letters but decide to go with the premise. Okay, you think, resistance is out. Acceptance is in. You close the computer so you can fully contemplate this notion of Acceptance. You stare in a meaningful way out the window.

Okay, Acceptance. The Hipster has left, but his cat is here. What is the lesson being offered by the Universe? Must you accept The Cat? Does this make The Cat The Hipster's proxy? Does this mean that what you're resisting in The Cat is actually yourself?

The Cat looks levelly at you, chewing the last of the cheddar with her sharp little teeth. Are you meant to see yourself reflected in The Cat? The Cat has resting cat face. Admittedly The Cat doesn't have a lot of facial options available to her. Still, you hate her.

That can't be good.

You reopen your computer, go straight to The Hipster's Facebook page, and there he is, smiling at you with his immaculately trimmed hipster beard. With a woman. Feeling a strange urge like that of the casual passer-by drawn to look at the scene of a horrific accident, you zoom in on their faces, until the awful truth reveals itself. The woman next to him is Rebecca from The Real Estate. They are at your favourite restaurant, not eating chickpeas from a can. They are both looking in an adorable manner at the camera.

You can't be sure, but she appears to be wearing a dress from your wardrobe. She probably stole it, along with The Hipster. You feel dizzy with self-pity. You pick up your phone. You have to ring him. The low-life rat fink.

Do not ring him. It will achieve nothing.

You close your computer.

How could he do this to you? Also, where did the phrase 'low-life rat fink' come from? It sounds like a sixties cartoon mouse villain.

Your thumb hovers over his number.

You put down the phone.

You reopen your computer, zoom back in on Rebecca from The Real Estate. She is thin. The Hipster likes his women thin. You had struggled to stay thin enough for him. The Cat has done you a favour eating the cheese. A hundred calories you won't be eating.

Rebecca from The Real Estate didn't know about The Cat. The flat doesn't allow pets. Perhaps you could go down to the restaurant with The Cat, hold her aloft and say, 'He lied to you. He owns a cat.' That'd kill the relationship stone dead.

Or maybe it wouldn't.

You wonder if Rebecca from The Real Estate has accepted that he still has his baby teeth, his adult teeth having never usurped the baby teeth's position. In this picture, however, his mouth is firmly shut, and she is planting a kiss on his bearded cheek, which is in close proximity to his teeth: proof she mustn't be put off by them. She has accepted his teeth. Good. Wait till she's spent thirteen months, two weeks and six days watching him eat with his tiny teeth. Let's see how she likes that.

The Cat, still sitting on the counter, is now licking one paw. You realise it was your looking at The Cat's sharp little incisors that reminded you of your ex partner's teeth. You wonder at the pointlessness of your thought process. You wonder at your life generally. You feel you haven't given enough contemplation to this Acceptance/Resistance Business.

You close your computer, put your right hand on your chest, feel the hammering of your heart. What exactly should you be Accepting? Rebecca from The Real Estate's duplicity? Liam from Finance purloining your idea? The Hipster's lying and philandering? The fact that, after all you endured and rationalised, it was he who left? The fact that you're thirty-three and eating chickpeas alone, with someone else's cat? What is the lesson the Universe has planned for you? There seem to be so many options.

You give the chickpeas a desultory stir on the coffee table in front of you and think, 'Get a grip on yourself, Kat. You do not need a man to be a whole person. You are a strong, independent woman with a good job and the stewardship of someone else's cat. You will develop a hobby. Diversify your interests.'

You wonder if Rebecca from The Real Estate has a hobby. You reopen your computer and, like a bloodhound on the scent of a wild boar, you find your way to Rebecca from The Real Estate's Facebook page. Her top post is a mythical-looking woman in a diaphanous dress atop a unicorn. The caption reads:

The Universe wants to give you what you want. Dream Big.
You just have to ask.

Clearly, Rebecca from The Real Estate asked for The Hipster.

Well, you're going to ask for him back. Two can play at that game.

You close your computer, put the uneaten chickpeas back in the fridge, and go down the three flights of stairs to the garden. You find the Gratitude Meditation Cushion lying forlornly underneath a grevillea. In a rare moment of anger, you'd thrown it at him. It missed him and went out the window, like in a sitcom.

'Finally,' he'd said, 'the mouse shows her claws.'

You had stood in front of him flexing your fingers in your pockets. You'd been tempted to correct the idiom and say, 'Do you mean "roars"? The mouse roars. She never shows her claws.'

You hadn't. You'd stood silently, frozen by indecision. Should you apologise for the pillow throw or return to the argument? You'd decided on the argument. You'd tried to keep your voice level and friendly. 'I'm sorry about the cows,' you'd said, 'but I don't want to eat vegan cheese. If you want to eat vegan cheese that's fine. It just doesn't taste like cheese.'

He'd looked at you intently, given you a tiny-teeth smile, picked up The Cat and the TV remote and walked out the front door. You were unaware that those were the last words you would say to his face. 'It just doesn't taste like cheese.'

You had sat on the couch waiting for him to return. After an hour, when the room had darkened, you'd called him.

No reply.

You'd called every hour on the hour until midnight. His voice-mail opened with an intimate 'Hi' that sounded like he'd picked up and was happy you'd rung. Your heart had been lifted and dumped eight times. You had rehearsed conversations in which you'd explained why his behaviour was childish and he'd apologised. You'd rehearsed conversations where he'd explained why your behaviour was childish and you'd apologised. If he would just pick up, you'd tell him you were fine with vegan cheese and you had a deep respect for cows.

He didn't pick up.

After a few days he had re-established communication through his friend Anton. Anton was very fit. It appeared he maintained this fitness by regularly bounding up your stairs to retrieve some item The Hipster claimed was his. Last time it was the coffee table. 'I think that's mine,' you'd said to Anton.

'Hey buddy, I'm just the removalist,' he'd said, swinging the table effortlessly onto his back.

You'd opened your mouth to restate your claim when to your utter shame, you'd begun to cry. 'Why did he leave me, Anton?' you'd sobbed. 'You're his friend. He must talk to you about me. Why did he leave me? What did I do wrong? He won't talk to me. Is he coming back? Tell him I'm fine with vegan cheese.'

Anton had stood there, frozen, like Atlas with the wrong prop.

This was understandable. Anton – having spent years staring at his *pectoralis major* surrounded by perfectly formed tiny lunging women with devastating eyelashes – was ill-equipped to deal with you. You were another beast entirely. You'd stood there hiccoughing, unbrushed hair like a male eighties rocker, trying to stop yourself from crying by pressing your fingers into your eye sockets. You were not in possession of long, camel-like eyelashes, so the net effect of the crying and the pressing was that you looked like a mole in shock.

'I don't know, buddy,' he'd ventured. 'I think maybe the relationship was a bit toxic... or not on the path... or road... or not your best self or something, or...' The explanation petered out and you stood looking at each other.

'Right,' you'd said, pulling an old tissue out of your pocket. 'Well, can you ask him why he took the washing machine and dryer? Those were mine. Also, why did he take the remote? It's not universal. It only works with my TV. I mean, did he mean to or was it accidental?' You'd loudly blown your nose and returned the tissue to your pocket. 'I sort of need it. Unless he took it because he's coming back?' you'd finished hopefully.

'Oh okay, so he took the remote,' said Anton, backing deftly through the door with the table. 'Well, buddy,' he continued, 'having to get up from the couch to change the channel is a bit of incidental exercise for you. He's done you a favour. Maybe think about doing some lunges on the way across the floor.' He'd demonstrated a couple of perfect lunges across the landing.

You still haven't bought another remote. You have to stand up physically, walk to the TV and fiddle with the buttons. The Cat on your lap dislikes being disturbed. You move across the room with her clinging to your arm like a sloth on a branch.

You tramp back up the stairs, put the Gratitude Meditation Cushion on the floor and sit on it. You can feel garden grit through your skirt. You accept the discomfort as a test of your focus on the job at hand. You're going to outdo Rebecca from The Real Estate with your Universe-recruiting technique. She doesn't know who she's dealing with.

You go for the direct approach. You speak aloud for extra Universe engagement.

'Dear Universe, kindly give me back The Hipster. Love, Kat.'

You lose confidence halfway through the statement. You're not sure if this is the tone you should be taking with the Universe. You might have subconsciously adopted the imperious attitude of The Cat. You go for a more consultative style.

'Look, Universe, he wasn't perfect, but as he said, neither am I. Yes, he had a temper but, as he said, I had difficulties expressing myself, so he was bound to lose patience with me. Maybe Thobra Khan is right? We attract someone to help us learn a lesson about ourselves. So, Universe, while we're chatting, is this what I'm meant to learn? That The Hipster was a reflection of my own unowned anger? But also, Universe, he was super food-fussy and I'm not, so what's that about? How am I reflected in that? Or is he reflected in me? Am I the part of him that loves dairy and sugar?'

You're tired now. You feel judged by The Cat. The whole med-itating thing could be too indirect. Also, what are you doing, going into a bidding war in the universal realm with Rebecca from The Real Estate? It's undignified. If she wants him, she can have him. Even though he's really funny, good looking and highly creative, he's also clearly disloyal and there is his temper thing. Though, in all fairness, you probably pushed him to it by being so indecisive.

Your phone is next to you on the floor. You pick it up. You scroll through your contacts. It stops on his number. It's a sign from the Universe.

Ring him. Just be upfront. Say Rebecca from The Real Estate looks like a cat-hater, and also you saw the remnants of a hamburger on her desk once, so how's that going to work?

No, don't humiliate yourself. You remove your thumb from the number. Anyway, you shouldn't 'Want'. You should be 'Grateful'. Maybe he's done you a huge favour? Maybe your soulmate is just around the corner?

You don't care. You can't stand it. You just want him back. You have to call him.

Do Not Call Him. Don't. Don't. Don't. Wait for him to call you.

You reopen your computer. Back to Facebook to distract yourself. Find yourself back at Rebecca from The Real Estate's page. A thin barefoot girl in rolled-up jeans stands on a jetty looking out over a misty lake. 'Life is ninety per cent what happens to you and ten per cent how you handle it,' the caption reads.

Actually, you misread it. 'Life is ten per cent what happens to you and ninety per cent how you handle it.' Well, Rebecca from The Real Estate's ten per cent includes procuring The Hipster, and yours includes forfeiting him, so it seems the ninety per cent is weighted in her direction.

'Chuck out any cats that aren't yours and go down to the bottle shop.' You may have made that up.

You look up. The Cat hasn't moved. She's probably nailed Mindfulness.

You shut the computer. You pick up the phone. You grab a pillow and scream into it to stop yourself from ringing him. This startles The Cat out of her Mindful state. You feel pleased.

The phone rings. You're so primed it sends a shockwave through your hand. It's his ring tone. Hope and anxiety jostle for primacy in your chest. Has the Universe heard you? He's calling to say 'sorry'. Or maybe he's not. You're holding the phone tightly in your hand like it's a grenade and if you release the pin it will go off.

Answer it.

Don't answer it.

Let him ring a few more times. You will your thumb to hit 'Decline'. Play hard to get.

You pick up. You say nothing.

'Hello,' he says.

A pause.

'Hello, Kat?'

You're like a reverse heavy breather.

'Kat, I just want to know if the cat's there?' Postmodern wanker never named The Cat. The call's about The Cat, not you.

Your heart is beating so loudly you're fearful he might hear it. Why did you pick up?

Why? Why? You feel sick with disappointment.

'Kat, is she, is the cat there?'

The Cat leaps off the couch and disappears out the window.

'No,' you say. Your thumb hits 'End'. You throw yourself onto the couch. You have to accept. Accept that he's seeing Rebecca from The Real Estate. Accept that you'd come home early a month ago and she'd emerged from a bedroom mould inspection with him in tow. Accept your own naivety. Accept that he was bored with you.

Accept you're not hot. Accept you were too pathetic to ask him why he took the remote. Accept that you were unable to keep him. Accept that he's more interested in The Cat than you, but you have an overwhelming desire to ring him back and admit that The Cat is here, tell him to come and get her. Stay the night. The gargantuan effort of restraining yourself exhausts you.

You go to the window, put the phone outside on the ledge, lock the window, go to the laundry and hide the key from yourself. There is a flaw in this plan, but your stress levels are so high you can't identify what it is.

You go back to the window to stare at the phone through the glass. The Cat appears through the gloom and sits on the outside ledge next to the phone. Doesn't meow. However, looks plaintively over her shoulder, contemplating her return to him.

'Please,' you mouth through the window. 'Wait there, I'll get the key.'

You trudge back down the hall, past the Deepak Chopra poster, formulating a plan as you walk. You'll buy her chicken. Then she'll stay.

STOP ASKING THE UNIVERSE FOR THINGS – IT DOESN'T CARE ABOUT YOU

Scroll through any social media news feed and you'll see the same 'self-help' sentiments repeated over and over again.

Live your best life.

Free your mind to control your destiny.

No dream is too big – abundance is yours.

You are a warrior woman, you deserve your own lion and cave.

(I may have made that up.)

The problem with these sayings is, as pretty as they are, their actual meaning is unclear. As we have seen already, if we really want to improve the quality of our lives across all contexts, we need to identify the cognitive flaws in our thinking. It's actually the key to any positive life change.

But this key is ordinary, plain brass. It's not jewel-encrusted or endorsed by a celebrity who's offering their own line of GMO-free probiotics so you can 'lead your best life'.

Some of the principles promoted by the self-help industry are, at their core, extremely valuable. If applied properly, they can help people lead better lives. However, they are often co-opted by unhappy people to justify staying in situations that are damaging to them.

Also, a lot of self-help principles are total rubbish.

So, let's look at how our brain glitches allow us to adopt philosophies that are unhelpful to our current situation.

The universe and more magical thinking

Kat's going through a breakup, and the whole miserable business is exacerbated by cognitive traps. Similar to the situation of hiring Lisa, her brain is leading her to make poor decisions. Her brain, like ours, is susceptible to dodgy ideas.

Kat's magical thinking has latched even more firmly onto the concept of 'the Universe'. Sitting in the aftermath of the breakup, she searches pointlessly for a lesson the universe might give her, and desperately tries to plug into the universe's wish-granting powers.

None of this is helpful. It can skew your thinking, doing more harm than good. The universe doesn't care about you. It doesn't plan life lessons for you. It will not give you what you want just because you've been thinking about it really hard.

We like to think the universe is something we can have a relationship with: that there's a special mystical undercurrent that can affect our lives. And there are many reasons why people believe this.

Sometimes things happen because you got lucky or unlucky. End of story.

We are social animals

The first reason people believe in the agency of the universe concept is that a whole lot of other people believe in it, too. We are influenced by those around us. We're social animals. Also, the simple act of understanding something makes us more likely to believe it. It's why people believe so many things that stretch credibility.

We can also develop a sense of belonging to a community based on shared ideas and ideology, which can harden those beliefs.

So, if someone has a lot of followers who talk about the power of the universe, then there's a collective inference that they're speaking the truth.

The underlying appeal of it, though, is that it can be really reassuring. There's a comforting notion that something is looking out for you. No matter how bad it gets, you're never alone. Second, it provides meaning when bad things happen. The idea that bad things can just happen for no reason is an unpalatable notion. There's no safety or encouragement in it. Believing that things happen for a reason, however, is much more soothing. Thinking that bad things happen to teach you a lesson that the universe has planned for you is fundamentally reassuring. It gives you a sense of order in chaos; a sense of control over your life.

A lot of this is subconscious. We don't start to believe in the universe or other implausible concepts because we consciously think they'll reassure us; it's under the surface.

More patternicity and confirmation bias

There are other flaws in our cognition that help us believe in the power of the universe.

The first three of these were covered in the previous chapter: magical thinking, patternicity and confirmation bias.

Magical thinking is where we believe that our internal world can affect the external world, and that we can magically influence the universe with our positive thinking.

Patternicity, where we see patterns in unrelated things, means we think we see 'lessons' the universe has planned for us, when they are actually just random, unrelated events happening. For example, we might think, 'I'm going to start thinking positively, which will mean I'm going to manifest more good things in my life,' and then we find $20 on the ground the next day and link the two. In actuality, it was complete luck.

The idea of manifesting something by thinking about it is nonsense.

Confirmation bias, the third cognitive flaw, makes us hyperfocus on 'this time', but forget the other fifteen times when we thought the same thing and nothing good happened.

Put the three flaws together, and we think we can 'see' the universe at work.

A new thing: hyperactive agency detection (HAAD)

We also have a natural tendency to ascribe agency. When things happen, we have an instinctive tendency to think something has caused it; that there is something making things happen; that there is an intentional agent. If we hear a metal gate creak open, our typical first reaction is 'someone opened it', rather than 'it opened in the wind'. This is another throwback to our dim, distant past: when there was a rustling in the bushes, it was safer to assume it was a lion than the wind.

We therefore break things into two categories subconsciously: things that are 'alive', as opposed to things that are 'not alive'. We're not talking biologically here: we're talking about something having sentience, or a mind of its own. In other words, when something happens, we think something intentionally made it so.

We ascribe agency to the universe in the same way. We think it can influence our lives. As reassuring as this notion is, you will make far better decisions, and leave damaging relationships and situations much sooner, if you unclutter your thinking and look the situation square in the face.

Argument from authority and charismatic people

The cherry on top is that the human brain has a propensity to believe other charismatic, powerful humans. It's called 'argument from authority'. Studies have found that we are more likely to agree to and believe something, even if it's wrong, if the argument is presented by someone who is authoritative and charismatic. When we're in the thrall of a charismatic person, we literally suspend our critical thinking.

Our social media feeds are littered with charismatic gurus and clueless celebrities mouthing simplistic, inspiring maxims that will apparently turn our lives around.

The halo effect

Our propensity to trust celebrities is extremely problematic. It's the by-product of the halo effect where, because we respect or like someone in one context, we infer capability on them in another. For example, think of an actress or model who we admire setting up shop on the internet and selling us vitamins or crystals. There's no shortage of charismatic, famous people keen to promote their extremely dubious philosophies and products. These products often have, at their core, some gussied-up psychological or spiritual notions, aided by some sciencey-sounding words. If the sciencey words hint at physics – or, even better, quantum physics – and give a general nod towards the concept of consciousness, the brain will be high-fiving itself for finding its way to the promised land of a fulfilled life.

Crystals are pretty, but they're just rocks. They offer
no healing benefits.

Why does it matter if people believe in this stuff? Well, while it might be comforting in a difficult situation to believe that the challenges you're experiencing are part of the universe's great plan, or that meditating on a crystal will improve your fortunes, it diverts your brain away from constructive problem-solving. Kat isn't thinking about the future; her brain is caught up in trying to figure out what lessons the universe has planned for her. She's trying to put the pieces together of a puzzle that doesn't exist, focusing and ultimately bargaining with an imaginary force.

Worse, though, it also clouds Kat's understanding of the situation and people involved. She should be looking at the situation with The Hipster realistically, focusing on the reality of his behaviour. She should be asking whether he was kind to her; whether he was loving, supportive and encouraging; whether there was equality in the relationship. She should be looking at whether there was a pattern to how he acted. She should be allowing herself to feel betrayed by his infidelity.

Instead, it's all framed in terms of inspirational slogans. She can't see the situation clearly, because all her magical thinking is getting in the way. It's clouding her judgement. She makes poor choices because of it. Long term, the bad choices accumulate and, before she knows it, ten years of her life will have passed by with her skewed intuitions running the show. Her rational brain so rarely gets a look in.

The gratitude and acceptance movement

Kat is looking at her situation through a lens of gratitude and acceptance: 'I should be grateful' and 'I must accept my reality.' This can be an immensely harmful way to look at things.

The self-help message around gratitude and acceptance is often aimed at women like Kat. It's not news that a lot of women struggle to assert power in relationships. Many woman have been pushed by their life circumstances into behaving in a submissive way. Is there anything more convenient to a submissive woman than the notion of acceptance, or the idea that wanting more is an expression of ingratitude? Add to this the unsubstantiated notion that the traits you dislike in other people represent unowned parts of yourself, and you're in some deeply unhelpful territory.

If you're in a relationship with another person – whether intimate, friendship or work – and an issue arises, there'll be something in the relationship dynamic contributing to the drama. But that doesn't mean the behaviour of the other person is an unowned part of yourself. That's unhelpful, simplistic and possibly dangerous. It's just another way to somehow make submissive people feel responsible for others' behaviour.

You don't have to accept or feel grateful for every situation in your life. If you want, you can get the hell out of there. If the other person is narcissistic, selfish or lazy, then you have every right to say, 'This is your stuff, not mine. See you later, buddy.'

Kat's appreciation of The Hipster's true nature is clouded by her ongoing negotiations with the universe. Yes, yes, some people need to put their grateful hat on before they launch their whinging selves into their day and create misery for their colleagues. If you have everything, and nothing's ever good enough, this is not your narrative. Stop reading it, and go and help a homeless person.

But if you're familiar with the notion of putting up with crappy behaviour and turning yourself inside out to be grateful, then read on.

Be grateful, sometimes...

The gratitude movement invites you to focus on the good things in your life and be grateful for them, rather than ruminating on the things that are not going your way. The notion of acceptance is complicated. In psychological terms, it's the idea of recognising your current reality and accepting it. According to Jon Kabat-Zinn, acceptance doesn't mean passive resignation. He says:

> *It takes a huge amount of fortitude and motivation to accept what is – especially when you don't like it – and then work wisely and effectively as best you possibly can with the circumstances you find yourself in... to mitigate, heal, redirect, and change what can be changed.*[1]

This sounds constructive, and it is. The premises of gratitude and acceptance are extremely worthy. Psychological researcher Professor Laurie Santos tells us having a gratitude practice is correlated with increased happiness and life satisfaction.[2]

However, the notions of gratitude and acceptance can be misconstrued, and it's then that they can become problematic. Being grateful for positive things in your life that you may be taking for granted is a worthy goal. However, trying to be grateful and accepting of things that are a blight in your life – not so much.

If you're a bit on the submissive side, or frightened of conflict, the idea of gratitude or acceptance provides a rationale for further

---

1   Kabat-Zinn, Jon (2006), *Coming to Our Senses: Healing Ourselves and the World Through Mindfulness*, Hachette Books.
2   Santos, Laurie (2021), 'The Happiness Lab' [podcast], happinesslab.fm.

submission. If your brain gets a whiff of a free pass on avoiding conflict by calling it acceptance, you get to appear as if you're holding the high moral ground – instead of being unable to hold your ground at all. It's easy to misconstrue the maxim and just accept all behaviours.

Particularly manipulative individuals can also misuse the principle and turn it back on other people. The notion of acceptance can become a tool to excuse harmful, hurtful and abusive behaviours.

In his excellent book *The Murder of Allison Baden-Clay*, David Murray noted that when police inspected Allison Baden-Clay's home after she'd been murdered by her husband, they found a 'gratitude diary' in which she had written about all the things she should be grateful for in her life.[3] This, while she was living with an abusive and finally murderous man. It's a perfect illustration of the misuse of a reasonable philosophy.

If your emotionally abusive partner has you convinced that it's not him or her, it's you, and you take a dive into the 'acceptance/grateful bucket', you're going to be inclined to justify their bad behaviour. In this way, the gratitude movement and acceptance principle are adopted as a mechanism for people to feel like they are in control. In a situation where someone feels powerless, the thing they *can* control is their own attitude. So, they choose to be grateful, to accept. It makes them feel like they are shaping their own life.

But it's only an illusion of power. And while they might feel in control, this false power can serve to do the opposite: it traps people.

If you're thinking to yourself, 'I've never even heard of this notion of acceptance or this gratitude ideology,' you'll still be

---

3   Murray, David (2014), *The Murder of Allison Baden-Clay*, Random House Australia.

susceptible to all sorts of theories and premises that need to be applied with care. Every time you go online and get hooked by a reasonable-sounding premise around diet, health, spirituality, politics, wealth creation – anything really – stop and ask yourself, 'Does it just *sound* valid? Are they using language that just *infers* credibility, or does it *actually* have value?' Approach all offers, ideas and theories with scepticism. Remember, we humans have a cognitive tendency to believe something merely because we understand it. So, if something simply *sounds* like it makes sense... beware!

Getting smarter

The universe doesn't care. It doesn't plan lessons for us, and it's not something we can magically influence with positive thinking. We have an inbuilt vulnerability to thinking the universe or something bigger than us might care, because of a set of brain glitches. But it doesn't, and thinking it does can scramble our judgement, making us unhappy and confused.

Worse, it stops us from actually dealing with our problems. And if you bring it together with the gratitude movement and acceptance principle – fine ideas on their own – it can help prop up harmful and abusive behaviours and relationships.

The question should not be 'What is this situation trying to teach me?' but 'What am I going to do about this situation?' We need to use our intellect, not have it relegated to the back seat in favour of our instinct and some vague notion of what the universe wants.

In trying to work out what the universe wants, we'll probably lean into our subconscious bias anyway and call it our intuition.

We need to be supported in honing our ability to make judgements about what we're told, and to build constructively on our own strengths. We need to discern, evaluate and learn to apply critical thinking to whatever the situation is. Seriously, we do.

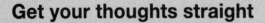

Get your thoughts straight

The Too-Willing Student

Are you assuming the current situation is trying to teach you a lesson? If so, remember it's not.

The Star Factor

Are you buying products or buying into philosophies because the person selling them sounds authoritative, or because they're famous in another context? Stop it.

Sounds Like Science

Are you buying products that have sciencey-sounding words attached to them, without proof of their efficacy? If so, stop buying them.

The Deity Delusion

Are you ascribing power to a hidden source?

The Gratitude Trap

Are you trying to put a positive spin on something or turn yourself inside out to be grateful for something, when actually you need to be taking action on the situation?

3

Kat meets the neighbours

There's a cat in the block. Mrs Hume has a sixth sense about these things. Not that she minds cats per se, but the body corporate rules are there for a reason. She suspects the couple in Flat Seven. They rent. Not that she minds renters per se, but renters have a different relationship with law and order.

Mrs Hume straightens her cardigan in the hall mirror, combs her grey bob, applies lipstick – noting the area of lip that requires coverage has diminished – arms herself with the body corporate agreement, double-deadlocks the door and heads downstairs, her arthritic knee slowing the descent.

She knocks discreetly but firmly on the door of Flat Seven. It's opened by the girl, a glass of wine in her hand. It's barely gone five.

Mrs Hume smiles, and hopes her face has taken on a pleasant aspect, while looking discreetly past the girl into the flat to validate her cat suspicions.

The girl doesn't return her smile and Mrs Hume readies herself for battle, but then the girl, in an act completely alien to Mrs Hume, throws her arms around her neck and bursts into loud, heaving sobs.

Mrs Hume barely knows the girl. She'd had to admonish her once about the position of her bin on the verge, but that's it.

The girl is thin but surprisingly strong. She clings onto her so fiercely that Mrs Hume feels slightly winded. She thinks it would be impolite to shift her position and worries that the respondent pressure she's applying is too light and tentative. She realises neither of them has spoken. Mrs Hume feels she should say something, or at least make a comforting noise. The girl's sobbing is echoing around the landing.

Mrs Hume is preparing herself to make the comforting noise when Mr Yee from Flat Nine opens his door to investigate. His English is terrible.

Mrs Hume disengages one arm and points to the girl while making a crying face to demonstrate that the girl is upset and she's comforting her.

He frowns. He's from China. He may not understand what's going on. She's not sure if crying is permitted in Asia. She wishes it wasn't here.

The door from Flat Eight opens and Mr Kovacic makes an appearance. It's now like Pitt Street Mall on the landing. Mr Kovacic, whose English is also disappointing, is of course irresistibly drawn to the drama. He, being Croatian, is well-versed in crying, yelling and all other forms of human expression. Mr Kovacic, his wife and his unmarried daughter conduct all conversations as if they were standing on the tarmac at Tullamarine.

Mrs Hume indicates with the same arm she'd used to clarify the situation to Mr Yee that all is well.

Ignoring her reassurance, Mr Kovacic begins traversing the landing, his big arms outstretched, and, to Mrs Hume's extreme discomfort, wraps her and the sobbing girl in a large hug.

'Oh, Kat,' he says to the girl.

Mrs Hume looks discreetly over her shoulder. Mr Yee, to her relief, remains in his doorway.

Mr Kovacic asks what the problem is.

Mrs Hume thinks this is intrusive. If the girl wanted to divulge the problem, she would have. Mrs Hume's shoulders are now damp from the girl's tears, and half a glass of shiraz is now trickling down her back.

The girl is composing herself to answer.

Mrs Hume wishes she'd hurry. Mr Kovacic smells. Mrs Kovacic should spend more time washing his shirts and less time yelling. Mrs Hume wants to go back to her flat to change her cardigan, but she doesn't know how to extricate herself.

'The cat has gone,' Kat whispers into the recently formed triumvirate.

I knew it, Mrs Hume thinks.

'Ah, Kat,' says Mr Kovacic reverentially. 'Big pussy run away.'

'Well,' Mrs Hume says, moving back onto the familiar and reassuring ground of regulations, 'you're not really meant to have one.'

Mr Kovacic, bringing a rich disregard of rules from his country of origin, looks disapprovingly at her.

The girl says, 'I didn't like her, but I miss her now she's gone.'

'Like my wife,' says Mr Kovacic. 'I don't like her, but I miss her when she goes to the shops.'

Mrs Hume thinks people should be more discreet about their personal lives.

'It wasn't my cat,' says the girl.

'I wish I could say the same about my wife,' says Mr Kovacic.

Mr Yee's wife, who, by the look of their mail, unaccountably has a different surname to Mr Yee, has now joined Mr Yee in their doorway. They are whispering quietly.

The girl's eyes are swollen, and mascara has run down her face in two rivulets. Mr Kovacic frees one arm to dab at her face with his handkerchief.

Mrs Hume uses the opportunity to free herself from the yoke of his arm. She's tempted to ask him to dab her back.

'Come in,' says the girl.

Mr Kovacic shadows Kat inside, tailed closely by Mrs Hume. Mr Yee and his wife follow in their slipstream and the entire group is now standing just inside her front door. Mrs Hume is not sure if Mr Yee and his wife were part of the invitation, but doesn't feel she has the authority to question their inclusion.

The flat is a disturbing combination of chaos and emptiness. The girl has no couch or coffee table, just two unpainted, splintered kitchen chairs positioned in front of the television.

'Where is boy?' asks Mr Kovacic.

'Gone,' says the girl, and begins sobbing again.

Mr Kovacic puts his arm around her and indicates, with an inclination of his head, that Mrs Hume should make some tea.

She feels this instruction is outside her remit, but in the spirit of neighbourliness she moves towards the sink. She wishes she hadn't. You could grow enough penicillin in it to fight a pandemic. Also, there's no kettle. What sort of person lives their life without a kettle? She boils the water in a pot. She tentatively opens the fridge. There is a limp cucumber, half a can of chickpeas, a takeaway container of indeterminate age and contents, and a container of milk. No wonder the girl is so thin and emotional. She's clearly an anorexic alcoholic.

Mrs Hume picks up the milk and sniffs tentatively. Surprisingly, it's fine. Probably for the wretched cat, she thinks.

Mr Yee and his wife are still standing just inside the front door. She offers them tea by a series of hand movements and the miming of a tea bag in a cup. They decline.

'Thank you,' says the girl, accepting the tea. 'You're very kind.' The girl gestures for her to sit in one of the two kitchen chairs. She hesitates. The girl says, 'My partner loved those chairs – said they were rustic.'

Mr Kovacic picks up one of the chairs and examines the underside. 'Boy is stupid. Chair is shit,' he says. 'I put out in council clean-up for you.'

The girl looks mournfully at the chairs.

Mrs Hume feels compelled to sit. She lowers herself warily. She is now uncomfortable as well as damp.

Abruptly, Mr Kovacic cups his hands and screams loudly in his native tongue in the direction of his flat. Mrs Kovacic screams back. The walls reverberate.

Mrs Hume indicates with her developing mime skills that Mr Yee or his wife should join her. She feels they should show solidarity with the uncomfortable sitting.

Again, they decline. They clearly don't drink tea or sit in company.

Two minutes later, Mrs Kovacic and her unmarried daughter bustle in, bearing a red kitchen chair and a bag of food. The unmarried daughter yells something at Mr Kovacic and deposits the chair. Mrs Kovacic puts the bag on the bench, kisses the girl on the cheek, moves to the sink, indicates to her unmarried daughter and Mr Yee's wife to join her, and commences cleaning. They all chat away in some Croatian–Chinese hybrid.

Mr Kovacic moves to the bench and starts unpacking the bag. 'Kat,' he says, putting a biscuit in his mouth. 'Eat, eat.'

'The cat,' the girl says, 'loved biscuits.'

'That's why big pussy is fat,' says Mr Kovacic, putting a biscuit into the girl's hand.

Mrs Hume is worried the girl is going to start crying again.

Mrs Kovacic turns from the sink and smiles. 'Don't be sad, Kat,' she says. 'The boy was a shit.'

Mr Yee's wife tuts in obvious agreement.

The unmarried daughter pauses in her task of wiping down the bench. 'You should come out for a drink with Helen and I, Kat,' she says. 'We'll get you smashed on a margarita or two.'

Mr Kovacic roars with laughter. 'Nika, one bad boy doesn't mean she doesn't like boys anymore,' he says.

'Settle down, Dad,' she says, flicking him with the tea towel. 'I'm just suggesting we take her out for a drink.'

Mrs Hume is quietly aghast. She had assumed the daughter's unmarried status was due to a lack of personal charm; now she has to consider a less palatable option.

Mrs Kovacic puts her arms around her daughter and kisses her on the cheek. 'Nika,' she says, 'this is lovely idea.'

Mr Kovacic walks towards Kat and puts a hand on her shoulder. 'Boy was bad bully, Kat. I hear him through the walls. Better he ran away.'

Kat turns to look at Mrs Kovacic and Mrs Yee, then looks up at Mr Kovacic, smiles sadly, and takes a small bite out of the biscuit.

A sensation arises in Mrs Hume's chest, like a foot being laced into a shoe two sizes too small. She places her hand discreetly onto her sternum, worried the heart attack she's feared is finally here. She glances at Mr Yee's wife, Mrs Kovacic and the Kovacics' unmarried daughter. Are they the last humans she will see? If she died, would they organise her a wake at the flats? Serve sauerkraut and black bean soup?

The lacing in the shoe tightens. Her heart constricts so fiercely she has to clutch the arm of the chair. She gasps and leans forward, astounded the others haven't noticed. She feels the panic rise as the lacing tugs so strongly her breath is forced up into her throat. Her vision narrows.

She focuses on the back of Mrs Kovacic at the sink, willing her to turn around, mouthing the word 'help', and, as if her will has compelled her, Mrs Kovacic, mid-plate-dry, turns.

But Mrs Kovacic doesn't look towards her. She looks at Kat. Mrs Hume watches through her diminishing circle of vision as Mrs Kovacic smiles warmly at Kat. Kat, accepting the offer of the clean plate, smiles back.

A sob trapped somewhere deep inside Mrs Hume escapes. The lacing around her heart loosens, the pain recedes, her vision clears, breath re-enters her lungs. She realises, in an epiphanous rush, that this is not the heart attack she had prepared for. This is not a physical condition. This is grief: grief for the lost years looking out at the world.

She wants to be among them. She's grieving for her lost place at the sink. She wants to be one with Mr Yee's wife and Mrs Kovacic; to plunge her hands, gloveless, into hot water; to know their first names; to stand with them, shoulder to shoulder, while they laugh at her poor attempts at Croatian and Chinese. To have them confide in her that the boy was a shit. To call her Lucy.

She comprehends that she is lonely. She aches for the hand of the daughter she never had to touch her on the shoulder.

Mrs Hume is now worried she may sob uncontrollably – perhaps outdo the girl. That would not be good. Mr Kovacic would want to involve her in another group hug.

She feels a soft touch on her shoulder. The Kovacics' unmarried daughter stands there, a cup of tea in her hand. 'You okay,

Mrs Hume?' she asks, handing her the cup. Mrs Hume looks up at her and is so struck by the warmth of her smile she reaches up and briefly squeezes her hand.

The front door squeaks open. They turn in unison towards it.

Mr Yee stands there, the cat in his arms.

'She hadn't gone far,' he says in remarkably good English. 'She missed you, Kat.' The cat looks uninterested.

The girl, taking the cat carefully from Mr Yee, smiles at Mrs Hume. 'I'm sorry, Mrs Hume. What did you come to see me about?'

Mrs Hume takes a large and shaky breath, rises from the seat and walks towards Kat and the cat. She scratches the cat behind the ear. 'Mr Hume was a vicious bully, Kat,' she says. 'He died ten years ago. I don't miss him.' Mrs Hume wonders at these words that have spilled from her mouth. She looks fixedly at the cat, feeling the warmth under her soft fur. She cannot move her gaze, for fear of what she'll see in her neighbours' faces. She senses the focus of the room shift; the molecules turn on their axis and settle around her. The air thickens and stills.

She holds her breath.

She hears footsteps, feels a tap on her arm.

Mrs Kovacic stands there, a tea towel in her hand. 'Here Mrs Hume,' she says. 'You want to wipe?'

The air thins, disperses.

Mrs Hume smiles and turns towards Mrs Kovacic. 'I do', she says. 'It's Lucy; call me Lucy.'

MRS HUME FROM FLAT TEN AND HER MENTAL SHORTCUTS

Okay, so you're probably looking at Mrs Hume and thinking, 'Typical old person, making racist judgements,' while you sit there shining your non-judgemental medal.

Well, not so fast, soldier. There are few reasons why Mrs Hume makes the erroneous judgements she does. There are things going on in her head that might be going on, at least to some degree, in your head too. It's the subconscious again. It's up to its old tricks.

Let's hear it for heuristics

The first trick is the heuristic.

What's a heuristic?

Glad you asked.

A heuristic is a mental shortcut. We need to be able to use a rule of thumb, an educated guess, to survive in our highly complex environment. The cognitive load (brain stress) required to think through every little decision from scratch would have rendered us obsolete as a race long ago, otherwise. We have survived via the use of heuristics.

We use mental shortcuts – heuristics – all the time. These cause generalisations in our thinking. It's when you think someone has a particular trait or behaviour because they are from a certain ethnic group or religion. They don't.

Think about generalisations. We humans love them. To a greater or lesser degree, we all stereotype. Stereotyping is adaptive. We need to make sense of the world by grouping things into broad categories. We know that a Border Collie and a Basenji are both dogs, even though they look different, because they both wag their tails and bark. Actually, the Basenji doesn't bark so that wasn't a good example, but you get my point. Mrs Hume is coming to her mostly subconscious decisions about the Yees and the Kovacics by using heuristics. We all do it.

The availability heuristic is a common cognitive bias whereby you draw conclusions about people or events based on information and memories that come most easily to mind. When Mrs Hume thinks about the Kovacics, the Kovacics' daughter, Kat and the Yees, she uses the availability heuristic. She makes assumptions about who they are based on her experiences or perceptions of people of the same ethnic origin, sexual orientation and age.

If you've ever been called a 'typical woman', you've also been pigeonholed by a brain under the influence of the availability heuristic.

Another example is how the media fills our brain space with news about disasters. If I asked you if the world is a more dangerous place now than it was a hundred years ago, you'd probably consider saying 'yes'. The data of course tells a different story: this is the safest time to be alive. If you want to investigate this notion further, read Hans Rosling's *Factfulness*, which details the reality of the improvement in the human condition over the past century. Yet our brains – constantly fed images of plane crashes, robberies and murders – make the incorrect assumption that we're hovering on the brink of disaster all the time.

Our attention is drawn to things that most easily come to mind. It appears more dangerous to fly in a plane than to get in a car because aeroplane disasters are more easily called to mind. However, getting in your car on your daily commute is a more dangerous activity, statistically speaking, than flying from Sydney to London.

We're tribal!

Yes, we're tribal! We all form conclusions about groups of people and endow them with stereotyped characteristics from a very early age. Whether our tribalism is based on region, ethnicity, sexuality, school, sporting team, political persuasion or social strata, there's a natural impulse to endow your own tribe with positive characteristics. 'We are the cool tribe and we are right. Other people who are not in our tribe are uncool, and definitely wrong. Probably about everything.' We can base our coolness and rightness on whatever context we want. People outside of our group are 'the others'. Not only the other, but very likely undesirable.

Not from our region? They probably have some pretty ordinary habits. Different religion, political persuasion or sexual orientation? They are definitely not going to be as righteous morally, or as generally right and reasonable, as us.

Remember, all this is happening subconsciously. Most of us don't get up in the morning with the intention of thinking ungenerous things about other people.

Also, in our skewed and subconscious perception of 'the other', other groups can become homogeneous, uniform – all apparently thinking and behaving the same way, with the same intention. Whereas 'our people' are all wildly individualistic, more interesting, and just generally all round a better quality of person.

Or so we think.

Of course, politicians cynically make use of this brain bias to convince people that outsiders are dangerous criminals intent on taking our jobs (and possibly murdering us in our beds).

We're better off being compassionate than empathetic

Uncomfortably, we're likely to be more empathetic towards our own tribe than 'outsiders'. This might seem like a non-problem but actually, empathy has a lot of limitations. If someone hurts one of 'our' people, we might be motivated to dish out some serious punishment. We are more likely to wreak revenge on anyone who we deem has hurt someone from 'our tribe'. This can make us punitive and overly emotional in our response. We can literally weaponise empathy.

Also, tempting though it may be, joining someone in their distress can be counterproductive. Once you've climbed inside someone's troubles with them it's much harder to actually help them, as you lose the advantage of emotional distance. Also, roaming around in someone else's pain can be exhausting.

There's evidence that having compassion is a better option. Compassion is where you're more likely to extend kindness to all people, not just your own tribe.

If you want to read more on the limits of empathy, read Paul Bloom's *Against Empathy*.[4]

Not everybody is born with the same opportunities.
Be kind. You don't know what people have been through.

---

4   Bloom, Paul (2016), *Against Empathy: The Case for Rational Compassion*, Ecco Press.

Also, as usual, some confirmation bias

Mrs Hume isn't setting out to be selective in her thinking. (None of us are. It's automatic.) She is also under the sway of our old friend confirmation bias – our capacity to only notice and remember things that confirm an already-held belief. The Yees, as represented in Mrs Hume's subconscious, are impassive, inscrutable and indifferent to learning English. She hasn't noticed, and therefore hasn't stored the memory, the times in the past when they've spoken English and demonstrated care and expression.

In Mrs Hume's preconception, the Kovacics are loud, hysterical and argumentative. She doesn't notice, and therefore doesn't store the memory, when they talk quietly and are conciliatory and kind.

Luckily, events can confront our subconscious bias and challenge unhelpful thinking. In the course of one afternoon, Mrs Hume's long-held and cherished beliefs – about renters, people who come from Croatia, people who come from China, people who have a different sexual orientation, people who break the rules and people who have cats – come in for some serious challenges.

The neighbours' kindness, the cross-cultural camaraderie and the Kovacics' non-judgemental attitude and emotional availability all cut across Mrs Hume's brittle self-defence, exposing her to the reality of being human and the complexity that entails.

This is often an emotional experience. Exposing someone to the humanity of 'the other' can blow apart their preconceptions. This is more powerful and persuasive than simply telling them that their thinking is wrong.

Stay connected to people. There's a lot of evidence that being plugged into a community is one of the most important things you can do for your health.

Getting smarter

The result of these cognitive biases is, of course, the judgements we make every day of our lives – both the small judgements we make about individuals, and the large, deeply troubling judgements we make about whole groups. It's easy to look at other people and see how generalised and judgemental they can be in their thinking; it's harder to look past our own heuristics.

Reacting is easy. Thinking is hard.

Get your thoughts straight

The Ism Assessment

Are you making an assessment of someone based on their ethnicity, age, socioeconomic status, sexual preference, accent, gender or political persuasion? Stop it. You have no idea who they are.

Take the Books Back to the Library

Are you loading yourself up with stories that tell you everything is going badly? Remember, we perceive things to be true when they most easily come to mind. If you consume media all day, it looks bad out there.

The Pros and Cons of Empathy

Empathy can be exhausting. Beware of climbing into other people's realities and swimming around in their pain with them. Remember, because we have a tribal brain, we're more likely to empathise with someone we perceive to be from your tribe. If you can, move towards a more compassionate place.

4

The Cat has a weight problem

You are fat.

Fat. Fat. Fat.

Since The Hipster left you two months, six days and fourteen hours ago, you've enjoyed a heroic amount of chardonnay; but now you've taken yourself in hand. Last week you lost half a kilo and executed a lame air punch in the bathroom.

The Cat was in the bathroom at the time, not weighing herself. She has a positive body image. If she could understand the principle of mirrors, she might not have. She's quite fat. You feed her a lot of chicken to ensure her continued tenancy. She has not, to the best of your knowledge, been on a juice fast and does not talk online to the Siamese next door about detoxing and clean eating.

You, however, have been 'clean eating' for six weeks. This current dietary phase was precipitated by an online article accompanied by before and after photos of a girl called Darcy Harrington. Darcy swore that her body's dramatic and rapid transformation was a result of getting back to nature. Organic, clean eating, juice fasting, detoxing and eschewing vaccinations.

Vaccinations were a plot by Big Pharma to fill your body with toxins and possibly make you autistic, said Darcy. If your body wasn't struggling with all the toxins caused by vaccinations, processed foods, dairy, gluten, sugar, chemicals and GMOs, it would naturally restore itself to its ideal weight. Our bodies were not designed for the toxic, unnatural environment we were forced to exist in, she said. She sat in front of the camera, in all her clear-skinned thinness, and spoke of how she'd been dieting for years but had finally stopped. Wanting to be thin was so yesterday. Darcy simply wanted to be healthy, fit and clean.

She certainly looked clean. And thin.

To be honest, you weren't that bothered about the healthy, clean thing, and your cousin had developed measles as an adult as a result of your aunt being a serious anti-vaxxer. He nearly died and didn't speak to your aunt for two years, so you think Darcy's anti-vax stance is seriously wacky too.

It was the thinness you were after. You'd imagined yourself in a month's time. You'd run into The Hipster at a club. He'd be amazed and stunned by your thin beauty. He'd want to buy you a drink and tell you how sorry he was, but he wouldn't be able to get near you, surrounded as you were by fawning, adoring men.

Your envious co-workers would gather around you and say, 'You look amazing.'

'Really?' you'd say, sipping your celery juice. 'Thanks, yes, I've lost three kilos.'

They'd ask how you did it and you would say, 'I just ate clean, and exercised more. It's not rocket science.'

Unfortunately, despite all the detoxing and clean eating, you've put the half kilo back on again since last week. You'd looked online for an explanation for this vengeful withholding of weight loss by your body, and the internet had reassuringly suggested it was probably fluid.

You hate fluid. Fluid is to blame for everything. Rain is fluid and it's wildly inconvenient.

You see very thin but surprisingly cheery Mrs Hume from Flat Ten at her newly instituted 'get to know your neighbours' dinners. Prior to her metamorphosis, your only dealings with her were in relation to the bin position on the verge. She would wait in the shadows at the side of the flats and watch you put the bin out. If its positioning was not to her liking, she would emerge, scowling, from the gloom, pointing one fairytale-crone gnarled finger at the offending bin.

However, since the night of your embarrassing breakdown on the landing, she's transformed. She's now the Good Witch of the flats. She bought you a kettle, feeds The Cat if you're late home, cooks you delicious high-calorie brownies and is constantly organising dinners.

At the last dinner, while Mr Kovacic, having tucked his military jacket into his track pants, drilled you all on Morse code, she had devoured her second piece of the Croatian cherry cake.

It was a long evening. By the end of it, you could all tap out your names and 'I need help, bring a medic' in Morse code. You suggested that a mobile phone could be quicker than tapping out Morse code on the wall, but Mr Kovacic looked at you severely and said, 'Kat, in a war, the first thing the enemy does is cut the telecommunication lines.'

'Settle down, Dad. We're in Sydney, not Dubrovnik,' said Nika.

A long discussion then ensued between Mr and Mrs Kovacic about how long canned goods last, in case of a breakdown in the social order.

During the discussion, Mrs Hume ate her third piece of Croatian cherry cake and another two pistachio biscuits. Thinness is wasted on the old.

You'd ask her how she stays thin, but you're worried she'll say she's usually fat but she's dying. She's been so kind to you of late that, if she was dying, you'd feel compelled to take care of her. You're worried you may not have the moral fortitude to care for the dying. So, you say nothing.

The Kovacics have a relaxed relationship towards food and Mrs Yee is Asian. Asians are all thin.

You wish you were Asian.

Take Amelia at work. She's thin. You asked her the other day how she did it.

'I can't keep weight on,' she'd said. 'No matter what I eat, it just goes straight through me.'

You'd wanted to stab her in the eyes with your quinoa and kale salad fork. Instead you said, 'Well, I think you look amazing.'

At which point she grimaced and said, 'You should try having to find clothes you like in a size four.'

She'd walked away on her little stick legs and you'd chewed on your quinoa and kale salad and imagined yourself calling out to the shop assistant, 'This size four is too big, do you have a two?'

Today, when you get to work, you're told it's Georgia's birthday. They're having cake in the communal area around the corner. 'It's chocolate mud,' says Thin Amelia.

This sends you into a spiralling panic. You love chocolate mud cake. If you approach the chocolate mud cake, you will be lost. Not only will you have the fluid-induced half a kilo to deal with, you'll also have potentially another kilo on top of that. It would be intolerable. 'I can't come,' you say. 'I've got a proposal to knock out before five.'

Thin Amelia's not buying it. 'Come on,' she says firmly. 'Georgia's new.'

You approach the communal area. There is the sugar-dairy-gluten-laden cake. There is New Georgia. She is also thin. At that moment, faintly overweight Jenny moves into view. You watch her trajectory, hoping she will join you at the cake table. But she deftly avoids it by waving her hands and indicating with a medley of facial expressions that she'd love to stay, but she's on the ropes with her project.

Damn her. Where's the solidarity?

You have now drawn parallel with the cake. You will only have a sliver. Just to be welcoming to Thin New Georgia.

'No,' says Thin New Georgia, 'have a decent piece. For god's sake, you only live once.'

It's true, you do only live once, and you've had an awful two months, five days and twenty hours since The Hipster left, taking the couch, juicer, kettle, Moroccan silver teapot and matching glasses, heater, washing machine, dryer, coffee table and TV remote with him. You'll get off the train three stations early tonight and walk. You'll get up at six tomorrow morning and go to the gym before work and only eat miso soup and rice crackers.

Two large pieces of cake later, you feel sick. The Hipster would have said, 'Serves you right for eating toxic sugar.' Fructose, the most evil of all sugars, never passed by his tiny teeth.

You are losing interest in your getting-off-three-stations-early plan. Your thin co-workers are now talking about going out for drinks and a Thai meal. A nice pad thai would offset the evil fructose, which has gummed up your mouth.

That evening, you are sitting in the back of a cab you can't afford, the thought of walking to the train station having defeated you. You look out the window of the cab and see a skinny stray dog scavenging his way through some garbage. His world is not one of a cornucopia of ever-available, delicious food. He is obviously doing intermittent fasting. With some success.

Intermittent fasting is clearly the way. The modern world is too replete with temptation. You are clearly eating too often. You must break the habit. You will go to a Pet Friendly Health Farm. You and The Cat will get back on track to health and fitness. After your stay at the Pet Friendly Health Farm, you will have established fabulous new habits. You will acclimatise The Cat to being walked on a lead. You'll be famous throughout the neighbourhood for being the Fit Woman with the Hilarious Cat Who Walks on a Lead.

If you can't find any Pet Friendly Health Farms, you'll raise the capital and open one. It will be a world first. Up in some Hinterlands somewhere. Healthy places where you can reclaim your Wellness are always set in Hinterlands.

The Cat will age gracefully, sitting in the foyer of the Pet Friendly Health Farm while you carry clients' luggage to their rooms effortlessly with your muscular arms. You and The Cat will be an inspiration to all guests and pets, combining brilliant business acumen, creative marketing and a hugely successful Top Ten Christmas gift book, *Wellness for You and Your Pet*.

Also, The Hipster will try to book in, but the Pet Friendly Health Farm will be booked out solidly for at least a year.

You arrive at the flats and get out of the cab. The Cat is staring at you from the lounge room window, blissfully unaware that her chicken ration is about to be halved.

You wave at her. She lifts a paw, places it on the glass. She's going to be a real winner at the Farm.

KAT'S NOT ACTUALLY FAT – NOT THAT THERE'S ANYTHING WRONG WITH BEING FAT

Alright people, we know that food is a tricky issue, so let's pick some of the issues in this chapter apart.

We need to talk about perfectionism...

Kat is not fat. Kat has a seriously skewed notion of how she should look. Whether or not she's overweight is not the point. Her unhelpful cognitive process is such that she constantly feels like she's failed. Her perfectionism – her impossible desire to be perfect – feeds the notion that if she doesn't adhere to an extreme diet, she may as well give up. She's constantly defeated by her own unrealistic expectations. If she eats something, she feels she shouldn't; instead of allowing her attention to move on, she fixates on it. It takes up an inappropriate amount of attention from her brain. She catastrophises that it's not just an errant moment, but disastrous.

In answer to this skewed response, she then sets herself up for further 'failure' by planning a punishing, unrealistic routine of exercise and restraint. Then, she berates herself when she doesn't stick to it, with the thought that she's weak and pathetic.

This judgement of herself keeps Kat trapped in the limbic system, going around and around in a pointless emotional circle. She's an all-or-nothing girl.

... and unrealistic expectations

It's not just food that trips us up when we are trying to meet unrealistic expectations. Study, exercise, managing our own behaviour, the expectations we perceive from others – perfectionism can trigger us at every turn. The fear of failure and judgement can be crippling. Kat needs to have realistic expectations of herself and set herself manageable goals, not swing wildly from one unattainable goal to the next.

That's easy to say, but when perfectionism has a grip on you, going for a rational response to the situation can be extremely challenging.

What's going on with your limbic system and food?

Let me introduce you to Miriam, your Paleolithic ancestor. Miriam and her friend Harriet have been roaming about the savannah looking for açaí superfood berries to lightly sauté back at their campsite. They are both hungry, having not eaten since yesterday lunchtime. With the light fading, they give up their literally fruitless search and head back to camp, where they are greeted by the smell of roasting impala. The fact the meat is roasted is a new and excellent improvement since Philip, Miriam's partner, accidentally discovered fire last Thursday.

It should be noted that they are not eating impala in sourdough bread – not because they've been reading Pete Evans and are on the Paleo diet, but because bread hasn't been invented yet.

Also, on that note, since their life expectancy is probably thirty, they shouldn't be rushing to get on the Paleo diet just yet.

So, they are sitting around eating as much roasted impala as their stomachs will hold, unconcerned that the fat hasn't been trimmed off. Not just because knives haven't been invented, but because they're not worried about eating fat, at all. They never think about it. Why? Because they might not eat again for a couple more days – or longer, if Philip's hunting party themselves are calorie deprived and therefore off their game. Literally. Miriam,

Harriet and Philip, and the rest of the group, are very driven to eat calorie-dense food. It means survival. The hypothalamus in the limbic system drives their hunger.

It did then. It does now.

Being driven by hunger was essential back then if we were to survive. Food was scarce and competition was stiff. When we did get to eat, we didn't sit around discussing what jus to serve it with. We didn't question whether we'd expended enough calories at the gym to eat the potato.

Fat and sugar, from whatever berries or fruits were available, were the bomb. We saw them, we ate them, we lived to see another day. The evolutionary drivers that motivated our forebears to eat calorie-dense foods whenever they presented themselves are still operating in our brains today.

So, Kat's frontal lobe, which is crucial in planning, is involved in a gargantuan battle with her limbic system. Our limbic system tends to view the chocolate cake, pad thai and glass of wine with the same urgency as we did the impala. It's up to the frontal lobe to explain that we don't need the chocolate cake, because we'll probably only be walking to the lift – not running for five hours to get a fig and a bit of papyrus root.

Unfortunately, the limbic system will often still triumph, making the decision to eat the cake; and then the frontal lobe will obediently post-rationalise our decision with the thought that we've had a hard week and deserve something sweet. Emotion versus reason.

Again.

So, we eat the wrong thing, we feel guilty, we go online and find some thin blonde who recommends the latest in diets. You know it has to be good because apparently everybody in Hollywood is doing it, and they all look great!

Let's have a word about the online diets, the appeal to nature, anti-vaxxers and also organic

We've all been on the internet and come across some new diet that sounded really promising because it had some sciencey-sounding words and it spruiked the notion that it was natural.

Anyone can have an opinion. Going on the internet and looking something up is not doing research. Proper research is conducted by specialists in their fields, and takes years.

Beware the word 'natural'. It's an umbrella term that means precisely nothing. There's a lot of noise about us all needing to be back in tune with nature. If we could just reacquaint ourselves with the beauty of the natural environment, all would be well.

In Hans Rosling's fabulous book *Factfulness*, he makes the point that nature is not something beautiful that we need to find our way back to or be in accordance with. For most of our existence, it's actually been trying to kill us.[5] Tsunamis are natural, as are earthquakes and hurricanes. Cancer is natural. Arsenic is natural. Death cap mushrooms are natural. If you wandered out into the bush and had a chew on some random plant, you'd probably find yourself sick, if not dead. Nature was not designed to serve humanity. Nature is dog eat dog. But the word 'natural' persists, representing the hallowed road to a healthy life.

Stop imagining a past that doesn't exist. Since 1900 life expectancy has more than doubled. Things were not better when we ate organic, natural food and treated ourselves with herbal medicines. We could die from a cut, and we didn't know germs were a thing.

---

5   Rosling, Hans (2018), *Factfulness: Ten Reasons We're Wrong About the World – and Why Things Are Better Than You Think*, Flatiron Books.

This is not to say that nature in all its facets is not a wondrous part of our existence; it's the use of the word 'natural' as a marketing tool that's problematic. When we think of the word 'natural', images come to mind of pristine forests, clear blue lakes, children frolicking in sun-filled meadows, their energy fuelled by plates of organic, natural oats. The word 'natural' is slathered on everything from dog food to moisturiser, and it's worth questioning what it actually means.

There's an implication that if we could just lead a natural, chemical-free existence we'd lead healthy, long lives. But would we?

Go and do a yoga class by all means, but just because someone can do a downward dog doesn't give them the authority to advise you on whether or not you should be vaccinating your child. Vaccines are responsible for the abolition of diseases that have come roaring back into life because of the madness of anti-vaxxers.

Get yourself and your children vaccinated. Also, vaccines don't cause autism.

We're using a heuristic when we think about chemicals

In chapter 3, Mrs Hume was using a heuristic – a mental shortcut – in her assessment of her neighbours.

When we're wading through health claims, we're equally as likely to put products with highly variable characteristics into the one convenient bucket. We have the 'chemicals' bucket (apparently bad) and the 'nature' bucket (apparently good). This generalised thinking makes it impossible to assess the information at hand.

Chemicals are in everything. If you've been spooked by the 'chemicals are toxic' message, go and look up the chemical makeup of a banana or blueberries. It's very reassuring.

Of course, there are huge problems with chemicals contaminating our environment. Pollution is a massive issue. However, the fact that *some* chemicals are bad and dangerous for humans and the environment doesn't mean they *all* are.

Organic foods are sitting neatly in the 'natural' bucket. They're marketed as pesticide free, but this is incorrect. They use so-called 'natural' pesticides, like copper sulphate and rotenone – which may be 'natural', but can also be toxic and do not require the same level of analysis as so-called 'unnatural' pesticides.

Our obsession with 'natural' is part of our desire to return to a previous era, when everything wasn't soaked in chemicals and we ate pure foods uncontaminated by processing.

But it should be kept in mind that only a hundred years ago, when presumably we were mostly eating these organic, clean, natural foods and relying on natural herbal remedies if we became ill, life expectancy was about fifty. A hundred years before that, it was forty.

Thanks to medical technology, improved food safety, education, improved sanitation and a thousand other developments brought about by science, we're now living to eighty-two.

Let's not listen to yoga teachers, cricketers' wives, alternative-health 'doctors' or thin, dieting girls on the internet when it comes to what we should be eating and drinking, and whether or not we should be vaccinating ourselves and our children. On that note, we should.

Do as much exercise as you can, as often as you can. It's unbelievably good for you. If they put all the benefits of exercise into a pill, they'd have the best-selling medicine on the planet. If you can do it in a gym, or somewhere else where you're exercising with people, even better. You get the social aspect along with the exercise.

Getting smarter

Next time you're contemplating going on a diet, remember that your limbic system is going to be in constant battle with your frontal lobe; and no matter how green, Paleo, organic, keto, non-GMO or intermittent it is, it's still your frontal lobe that has to convince you, day-in and day-out, not to eat the chocolate.

Give yourself a break. Your brain is not on your side when it comes to trying to control your eating. And anyway, a lot of the diets are pseudoscience and are dead wrong and stupid.

The words 'ancient', 'traditional' and 'natural' should all be viewed through a sceptical lens.

Even if you're not obsessed with the latest dietary fad, that doesn't mean eating sensibly is easy. So, beware of setting yourself up for failure. Try to set yourself reasonable goals that you have some chance of achieving – because at the end of the day, your brain is going to take a lot of convincing.

And finally, I know I'm diving into a huge pool of social expectations, but it's probably worth asking yourself what's driving your need for weight loss, and whether it is reasonable. Who knows, you might discover you're fine just the way you are. What an astonishing proposition!

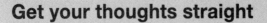

Get your thoughts straight

Loosen the Corset

If you're redoing tasks because you fear they're not perfect, you're in the grip of perfectionism. Send the proposal. Do the presentation. Allow employees to take full responsibility for something without you having to compulsively recheck their work.

Dump the Diet

If you are prone to setting yourself unrealistic goals in relation to dieting, see if you can approach your health from a more practical place. Make a note of how much of your mental energy is chewed up thinking about your food consumption. Consider what else you could be doing with your brain if that time was freed up. You're on a hiding to nothing because your limbic system is not on your side.

Trolley Tracking

Make a note of your voyage down the supermarket aisle. How much critical thinking are you applying to your shopping? Words to be suspicious of include: 'natural', 'diet', 'organic', 'GMO free', 'gluten free' (unless you're a coeliac), 'low fat', 'no preservatives', 'chemical free'.

The Pedestal Effect

Do you buy products because a celebrity you like endorses them? Stop it.

5

Kat has a meeting

You are in the playground. Lunchtime. You are waiting for your turn to skip into the rope that's being held by two other children: Tyler Kaplan and Janet Kraft.

Alexandra Finch is ahead of you, and Toby Cooper is behind. You are sandwiched between the two most popular kids in your year. The rope is being turned quickly. Alexandra Finch has just leapt confidently into the rope, without hesitation. She is jumping flawlessly in time with the chanting, and still finding the time to laugh engagingly. The sun is glinting off her blonde bob. She effortlessly exits the game after ten immaculate jumps.

You arrive at the rope. Your heart is beating out of your chest, your hands are sweaty and you think you might vomit. The rope is a rapid blur. You spread your arms, bob with each turn of the rope, but it's moving so quickly your opportunity keeps passing you by.

Alexandra Finch has now taken over rope-turning duty from Janet Kraft, whose arms have tired. Alexandra Finch has unflagging energy.

Go, you say to yourself. Just go, Kat. Go. Go. Go.

Three, four more times the rope turns, and three, four more times you lean towards it, desperate to prove you can do it. Your legs are so shaky you're terrified they'll get tangled. You will fall. The game will stop. Everyone will think you're hopeless. You stand there, sweating, your heart now beating so loudly you're sure everyone will hear it. You're frozen with fear, miserably baulking at the rope.

Jump, you say to yourself. Just jump, Kat. Just jump.

Speak. Speak, Kat. Just speak. Go on, Kat. Speak. Speak. Just say it.

You are in a meeting.

It's been four months, five days and eighteen hours since The Hipster left. The office table is scattered with half-drunk takeaway coffee cups and empty cupcake shells. There's an inspirational poster on the wall.

Make your life a Masterpiece. Imagine no limitations on what you can be, have or do.

Inspirational sayings dog you wherever you go. You don't feel your life is a masterpiece – more like a crayon drawing made by an exhausted post-tantrum four-year-old.

It's Peter from Marketing's birthday. You all sang a half-hearted, off-key 'Happy Birthday' at the beginning of the meeting. You've been sitting in the meeting now for twenty-six minutes and forty-seven seconds. You know this because your Fitbit is telling you. Your Fitbit was a birthday present from your neighbours. You didn't know old people even knew such things existed. Mrs Hume presented it to you at a dinner cooked by Mrs Kovacic and Nika. Since The Hipster left, the neighbours are constantly asking you to dinner. It's probably why you can't lose the 2.75 kilos. They all took turns trying the Fitbit on. Mrs Yee's *resting* heart rate was fifty-two.

The Hipster's resting heart rate had been fifty. He'd said it was because of his commitment to meditation and mindfulness, and that all stressors were the Universe offering you the opportunity to remain calm.

However, it seemed that not being able to find the TV remote had been outside the Universe's syllabus. You would re-enter the lounge room once his raging at your inability to 'simply' put the remote back in the correct place petered out. You would find him sprawled on the lounge, one foot on the floor, flicking through the channels. He would turn towards you, smile, proffer a beer, but no apology for the screaming. Like you'd imagined the whole episode.

'You found the remote?' you'd venture.

'Yeah, babe. Yeah, all good,' he'd say.

The Cat, stiff with disapproval, would stalk past him.

You would accept the proffered beer and stand behind him looking blankly at the TV, your knees pressed into the couch. You were too shaken to tell him you always put the remote back – it was him who always lost track of it, after a few beers.

Back in the meeting, your resting heart rate is currently tracking between seventy-five and ninety-three, actually ninety-four. That's not good. Also, is it really a resting heart rate if you're in a meeting with plagiarising Liam from Finance?

You check your Fitbit again. You've only done three thousand seven hundred and sixty-eight steps. You are regretting not putting the Fitbit back on for an hour after your shower this morning, so you're mentally giving yourself another thousand steps. If it's not recorded, though, it doesn't count. Like life, really.

You've gone to speak six times in the past twenty-six minutes.

Actually, now twenty-seven minutes and thirty-eight seconds.

The meeting is only slated for an hour. You have thirty-three minutes and twenty-two seconds left in which to speak. Your heart is slamming against your ribs, your hands are sweaty and you feel sick. What is wrong with you? It's just a meeting. Just speak.

Laura from Legal has just started speaking. She has lovely hair, but you find her cold. She has one of those quiet voices that commands attention. People have stopped looking at their phones and are looking intently at her.

You are quietly spoken as well, but people don't look so much *at* you as *through* you. You know your own hair is marvellous, but Laura is also very slim. Slim but remote. You estimate fifty-eight kilos, which at one hundred and seventy-five centimetres tall is optimum. You've seen her tap across the foyer in her workout gear and cycling shoes in the morning. People shouldn't parade themselves around when their colleagues are trying to cram a cinnamon scroll in their mouth at the cafe downstairs to keep their energy up before the long day ahead.

She's currently punctuating her well-thought-out points with her attractive hands. She is wearing a Fitbit, too.

You would give anything to see her step count.

You wonder if she has those scales that don't just tell you your weight, they tell you about fat and water percentages, too. You slump further in your seat and check your Fitbit again. The Hipster didn't approve of wearable devices. Or, really, any devices. Or appliances.

He thought modern society was killing us with its chemicals, processed foods and pharmaceuticals. He talked about living off the grid, in a hut made of logs he'd hand-hewn. You'd apparently be eating organic oats and spinach, which you'd lovingly tended from dawn to dusk on your seven-hectare property. You had imagined yourself in some sort of frontier dress with an apron, your hand resting on a white picket gate, your Victorian messy-bun hair glinting in the late afternoon sunshine. Then you'd remembered you disliked the country and had no gardening interest or skills.

You'd smiled encouragingly anyway, while imagining the horror of no coffee or cinnamon scrolls. Still, you'd thought, you'd be thin!

Back in the meeting. Twenty-two minutes, forty-five seconds to go.

No step increases.

Sometimes your Fitbit mistakes arm movement for steps.

Not today though.

Also, you still haven't spoken. Every time you attempt to, you break out in a sweat.

Simon, your manager, gave you feedback at your last performance review. 'You're a bit too reticent, Kat. You've got good ideas. Let's hear some of them.'

The Hipster, in the last couple of months before he left with Rebecca from The Real Estate, used to give you feedback on being too tentative. 'Come on, Kat, argue with me. Tell me what you think.'

This was a trap. Even mildly disagreeing with him resulted in him giving you a tight smile with his tiny teeth on display, and a look as warm as a frozen tundra.

What if you open your mouth and your opinion is under par? Stop being negative, Kat. Stop putting yourself down. Be positive.

You take yourself in hand. Give yourself a mental slap across the cheek. Stop being so pathetic, Kat. Just open your mouth and say it. You sit up in your seat. Reframe the opening sentence. Decide to start with 'These measures are,' as opposed to the more insipid, 'I think there are some issues.'

You take two calming, deep breaths, which don't work. You inhale for a third time, slowly. You're building up to it, you're going to jump, one more second and you're there.

You're about to do it. You inhale, lean forward.

Toby Cooper taps you on the shoulder. 'Gis a go, Kat.'

He moves past you and jumps without preamble into the rope.

Your mouth is forming the word. 'These...'

Too late. Peter from Marketing is speaking. He has no qualms about expressing himself.

Words come spilling out of his mouth in torrents. He seems much admired.

You don't admire him. Even though it's his birthday, you're finding it hard to look at him in an interested way. He uses the words 'synergy' and 'passion' relentlessly, which you loathe. Also, his ideas are completely bereft of originality. So much for innovating.

Heart rate now one hundred and ten. You need to exercise more. If you got off the train one station early, you'd get your steps up. You could start cycling. You'd have to attach the Fitbit to your shoes though, so the wheel revolutions would count as steps.

You look up. James and Matthew have apparently been speaking after Peter. They've done a dual graph on the whiteboard. While you'd been strategising around your steps, you missed the presentation from the three disciples.

Nine minutes, twenty-three seconds to go. It's too late to speak now. You'll look desperate. The upside of that, though, is that nobody can judge you. That's a good thing. Judgement is awful. You invariably fall short.

Actually, in all truth, it's not just negative judgement you're afraid of, it's people being stopped in their tracks by your incisive comments and quiet, understated gravitas.

Maybe you didn't speak, but at least you didn't out yourself as being mediocre.

You unclench your hands and begin to close your redundant notepad.

You walk away miserably. A tap on your shoulder. It's Alexandra Finch. 'Kat,' she says, taking your hand, 'I'll jump with you.'

You hesitate. Pivot. Comply. You move in tandem across the playground. You arrive at the rope. She grips your hand more tightly and leaps. You leap with her.

Laura from Legal is speaking. Again. Why doesn't she filibuster for a living?

'I read an analysis of the project written by Kat,' Laura from Legal is saying. 'I thought her assessment of the issue was incredibly accurate. Kat,' she adds, 'why don't you give a summary of your assessment?' She smiles at you warmly.

Seven minutes thirty-six seconds to go. You look at her. Smile. You regret the cold, remote, filibuster judgement. You rise, reopen your notebook. You start to speak. You are speaking. You are jumping. Alexandra has let go of your hand. The children are chanting. The fear transmutes seamlessly into exhilaration. You jump high, feel the whir of the rope fly past your legs. The bell rings.

You could jump for ever.

IF YOU HAVE TROUBLE SPEAKING IN MEETINGS, THIS IS PROBABLY WHY

Anxiety is just about the most common mental-health issue around. And while we might not call it anxiety, we all experience fear sometimes. Sometimes the anxiety or fear we feel surprises us by its intensity and can seem wildly disproportionate to the event.

On top of the fear, there's a lot of expectation that we should be positive and living our dreams.

> *Just Do It!*
>
> *Climb that mountain!*
>
> *Fight that bear!*
>
> *Leave that crappy relationship!*
>
> *Speak up in that meeting!*
>
> *Live your best life!*

So, let's look at what's driving it and what we can do about it.

Miriam and her friend Harriet are out on the savannah again!

Miriam and her friend Harriet, who were having difficulty finding açaí superfood berries back in chapter 4, are out on the savannah again. They hear a rustling in the bushes. Let's see how the limbic system and the frontal lobe respond to the noise.

We've all heard of the fight-flight-freeze response. Miriam and Harriet's limbic systems interpret the rustling as dangerous.

In response, their two amygdalae – the part of their limbic system that responds to fear – release a cascade of chemicals to prepare them to do one of three things:

1. *Fight:* as in going into battle.
2. *Flight:* as in running as fast as you can.
3. *Freeze:* as in a rabbit in a headlight.

So, the rustling happens in the bush just to the left of Miriam. Before her frontal lobe has time to reason out the possibilities – whether it's just a light breeze, or a lion – her limbic system assumes 'lion' and triggers a flight response. So, she runs away, scattering precious berries as she goes.

When Harriet's limbic system fires off, she is triggered into a freeze response. She stands dead still, holding her breath, in the mistaken hope that the lion won't see her.

The lion sees her. There'll be no lightly sautéed superfood berries or roasted impala for Harriet that night – or ever.

Miriam kept running, and lived to forty-six. Her limbic system kept her alive long enough for her to have progeny, and then they had progeny, and on and on until you were born and are reading this. Her friend Harriet never got the chance to create progeny, so your friend Eloise never had a chance to exist. Shame, as she would have been nice and a pretty good laugh.

The point is your brain, and Kat's brain, contains the same operating system as Miriam's and Harriet's. Our amygdalae are likely to be triggered in the same way as theirs. Your brain could interpret any of the following contexts as equal provocation for a fight, flight or freeze response, just as the rustling in the bushes did for Miriam and Harriet:

- You're presenting to the board.
- You're about to go into an interview.

- You walk into a networking event.
- You have to jump into a skipping rope at school.
- You have to speak up in a meeting.
- You walk into a party.
- You're about to meet your in-laws for the first time.
- Someone yells at you.
- Someone asks you to marry them at the same moment you were about to break up with them.

There are obviously thousands more contexts in which your fight-flight-freeze response can be activated. Once the activation has taken place, a cocktail of chemicals causes a series of inconvenient physical symptoms, which you may find familiar. These include racing thoughts, increased heart rate, elevated blood pressure and sweaty palms. You might also develop dry mouth, butterflies in the stomach and nausea. These responses are due to your body diverting blood flow from the digestive system to the mechanisms that support you to go into fight-flight-freeze. In other words, out of nowhere you find yourself a sweaty, nauseated, incoherent mess. It's all very inconvenient.

The problem is, we are living in a modern environment with a brain that's designed for darker, more dangerous days. Our limbic system is frequently wide of the mark. Approaching someone you don't know at a party may well fire off your limbic system's anxiety response, but this is the moment you need to use your critical-thinking skills.

What to do when you find yourself in fight-flight-freeze

When the inevitable happens and you find yourself in fight-flight-freeze, here's what to do.

1. Acknowledge that you're in the grip of a fight-flight-freeze response.

2. Don't judge yourself. Avoid giving yourself a hard time. Watch your self-talk. Is it saying, 'Oh look, there I am again. I'm such an idiot for getting myself in this state. Just relax'? Telling yourself to relax and criticising yourself doesn't help – it just keeps you trapped in your limbic system.

3. Divert your attention. You need to get your cognitive process out of the limbic system and into the frontal lobe. You could:

   - Count backwards from three hundred by sevens.

   - Spell your name backwards.

   - Find something in the environment you can focus on. Look out the window. Is a plane flying overhead? If so, you can wonder where the plane is going, and who might be on it.

   - Look at a piece of jewellery on the person opposite you. Really examine it. Is it gold? Is there a pattern? Don't, however, stare at them in a creepy manner.

   - Do anything else that gets your thinking out of the spooked part of your brain and into the rational part of your brain.

4. Gently challenge the reality of the danger in the situation. For example, 'I'm about to speak in a meeting. This has made me anxious. This is understandable. However, the reality is I know what I'm talking about and my opinions are worth listening to.'

5. Go back to what you were doing. Speak up in the meeting. Break into the group at the party. Do whatever it is that's spooking you. That is pretty much the only way through. The more you do things that scare you, the easier they become.

6. After the scary thing is done, congratulate yourself, and make a mental note that you didn't die. That's always a bonus.

Another thing you can do if you're in a limbic-system spin-out is to eat something. Obviously, not a three-course meal – but something small. This engages your digestive system, which is shut down during the fight-flight-freeze response to prepare you for action. If your digestive system is up and running, it's difficult for your limbic system to stay in a state of heightened arousal.

Don't, however, set yourself up for failure. Being a human is complicated. Give yourself a break.

When to go with the fight-flight-freeze response

If the situation arises that you're alone in a car park late at night and you hear a noise, or you're about to get into a lift and you get an uncomfortable feeling about the lone person already in there, or you're at a party and the person you're talking to offers you a lift but something feels amiss, respect that feeling. Do *not* analyse this. Just take action. Don't get in the lift. It doesn't matter if it's a false positive; better safe than sorry.

Remember that your subconscious is scanning the environment all the time, looking for potential signs of danger. We are unaware of this most of the time. We'd be unable to function if we consciously had to process everything our subconscious is picking up. So, this is where our intuition should definitely be respected.

Perfectionism is driving that fight-flight-freeze response

As in chapter 4, Kat's perfectionism is at it again. It feels justified. In conversation, she would defend her need to achieve perfection. She is unwilling to speak until she can guarantee the words coming out will be perfect. The perfectionism is its own suffocating corset. She runs a continuous track of negative thoughts, which support the notion that her contribution will be second rate. She feels that perfection is required, and this belief descends deeply into her subconscious.

Watch out for being perfectionistic. Great is the enemy of good.

As Michael Shermer says in his book *How We Believe*, belief comes first, and reason comes second.[6] Not only does Kat have a fundamental and emotional belief that her contribution will be suboptimal, but her conscious mind is also manufacturing logical evidence as proof that this is true.

Again, in order to counter this, we need to challenge these unhelpful beliefs with critical thinking. I hope you're beginning to see how much we need to counter these presumptions that are generated in the emotional part of our brains! Who knows? You might even come up with some positive things to think about yourself.

Amazing.

Heuristics at work again

Just like Mrs Hume's assessment of her neighbours in chapter 3, Kat's using a heuristic – a mental shortcut that leads her to conclude that, since Laura is a well-presented, quietly spoken, slim, attractive lawyer, she must be cold and competitive. Confirmation bias kicks in, which confirms her intuitive assessment. Time and

---

6   Shermer, Michael (2003), *How We Believe: Science, Skepticism, and the Search for God*, Holt Paperbacks.

time again we are more likely to only see what we expect to see. Laura's kindness forces Kat to reassess. This shows us that, if we're open to having our minds changed, something in the environment can provoke us into some critical thinking. If Kat's lucky, she may learn from this and be less likely to jump to incorrect conclusions in the future.

Your memories are probably wrong

Somewhere in our subconscious, we carry the echoes of events from our lives. If these events were negative, we are more likely to remember them. When a situation arises that has similar elements to a previous event, it can trigger the memory. Maybe we won't remember the actual event, but the flavour of the incident may resurface. This can easily influence our current behaviour if we're not aware of it.

There's a theory that memory is not actually about love and fear and retaining beautiful memories to cherish as we descend into our dotage; it's actually about survival. We remember things so we can guard ourselves from them happening again. Negative, highly charged events leave a post-it note on the whiteboard of our brains. Our internal post-it notes say helpful things like, 'Remember that party you were at in 2015 where you stood with one drink for two hours in the one spot, spoke to no-one, then went home? That's probably going to happen tonight.'

We are more likely to recall negative events than positive. Kat has remembered the agony of not jumping into the rope, but Alexandra's kindness is more deeply buried.

Getting smarter

We are under a lot of pressure to perform. There's no shortage of books, podcasts and seminars helpfully telling us that, if we think positively, the world will be ours. But with our amygdalae firing off our fear responses, our perfectionism tells us whatever we're attempting is not good enough and our memories layer on some unhelpful scenarios. No wonder we struggle to 'Live our Best Life' and 'Be our Best Self'!

Without understanding the process our brains are going through, these pointless motivational statements just serve to further the feeling that we're failing. The implication is that, if we could just get our attitude right, we'd be winning.

Our brains are thwarting our attempts to find our voices and take action when we're under pressure.

Watch yourself hold your breath and stay very still, in a sub-conscious attempt to render yourself invisible, next time you're in a meeting and you don't want to be asked a question. You, like Kat at the skipping rope, have gone into freeze mode.

One of the most serious ramifications of being under the influence of the fight-flight-freeze response is that women who have been sexually assaulted are accused of lying, as they didn't try to stop the assault or call out for help. We now understand that under such a serious threat, it is very common to go into freeze mode and be unable to move or scream.

So, back to performance anxiety. In any context it can be a nightmare. Berating yourself for not thinking positively enough or not being braver is just unhelpful. If you're struggling, that's okay – your brain is presenting you with some formidable barriers to overcome.

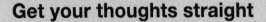

Get your thoughts straight

Tame the Dragon

You're going to get triggered – no two ways around it. Something or someone is going to ruin your equanimity. Once you're aware you've been triggered, try to take the steps outlined on pages 87 and 88.

No Thanks for the Memory

Our memories are unreliable. If you're in the middle of an argument and you find yourself about to say: 'I absolutely remember clearly saying to you...', then maybe don't say it. You could well be wrong.

Books and Covers

We've all been told at some point not to judge a book by its cover. Turns out, it's top advice. Watch for judging someone based on your gut response, especially if it's to do with their appearance.

6

Kat has a performance review

Today is your performance review. The invitation popped up last Thursday. As far as you're concerned, the word 'invitation' should be sequestered for happy usage, like weddings and makeup events at David Jones – not dispiriting performance reviews.

Your manager, Simon, is conducting the review. Simon reminds you of your Uncle Steve, who's also had a fairly tragic hair transplant. Simon's hair implants are recent, so his hairline is reminiscent of a reforestation project.

Your plan for the performance review is to get in and out without having to talk about why you hired Lisa Miles, who was brilliant in the interview but since then has revealed herself to be Satan with Good Hair. Between Lisa and The Hipster, your life has virtually been ruined.

You reach into your bag and pull out a bottle of breath freshener, spray it into your mouth and immediately gag. You look at the bottle. It's lens cleaner. Why do they make the bottle so similar? Surely myopia and halitosis are not such rare companions.

You have to walk past Lisa Miles' desk to get to the office in which your review is being held. Normally you avoid this route at all costs. She looks up as you pass. Smiles faintly. Tucks an imaginary escaped hair behind her ear. 'Good luck with your performance review, Kat.' She, like Putin, knows everything about everybody.

Simon is there before you. It's a window-facing office. Good. The internal offices make you claustrophobic. Simon is on the phone when you arrive, and with a theatrical wave, indicates the seat. His eyes are blue and clear, framed by well-tended eyebrows. Men with overly groomed facial hair make you uncomfortable. The Hipster's eyebrows were invigoratingly wild and masculine.

You run two fingers over your own unkempt eyebrows.

'So, Kat,' Simon says loudly, as if the room were full of people and he must speak over the din, 'how are you?'

'I'm good, thanks, how are you Simon?'

'I'm well thanks, Kat. Glad the heat's behind us. My wife says it's been the hottest summer she can remember. I'm not sure about that,' he says conspiratorially, 'I think it might be her age.'

You didn't even know he was married. Now your mind is constructing poor menopausal Mrs Walker.

'Do you play sport, Kat?'

Oh god, you think, he's creating rapport. 'I go to the gym, Simon.'

'Oh, well, that's very good, Kat. Keeping fit is very important. Though saying that, the extent of my sport involvement is watching my son play soccer.'

You loathe all sport but are now compelled to ask him how old his son is and in what position he plays.

'He's eleven, and he's a striker,' says Simon.

'Striker, Simon,' you say. 'Well, that's impressive.'

You and The Cat were pressed into service as soccer-mad friends to The Hipster during the World Cup. You had feigned interest and risen at 4 am, to sit, freezing, on the couch. Mr Kovacic, immune to the early hour, would materialise in his red-and-white-chequered dressing gown, deposit Croatian fritters and Ožujsko beers on the table, pat you on the head and take up his position ten centimetres from the TV. The serious shouting would then commence. If their railing at the clearly biased and corrupt refereeing became too vocal, Mrs Kovacic would rap sharply on the wall. The chastened Mr Kovacic would then sit on the couch, put 'big pussy' on his lap and obediently clap his hand over his mouth to muffle his gusts of horror or triumph. The Hipster would shake his head behind Mr Kovacic's back, and mouth 'stupid Leb'. You did not consider Mr Kovacic a stupid Leb, but would nod in tacit agreement.

'So, Kat, what achievements are you most proud of?'

Well, you're not proud of being mean about Mr Kovacic. Concentrate, Kat. Bring this review to a close. You put your hand to your chin, like you're really considering the answer.

'Well, the team hit its KPIs.'

He looks down at his papers. 'Good. Yes, I can see that. So, what are your goals for the next six months?'

Your goals are losing 2.75 kilos and getting The Hipster back. 'I plan on consolidating the progress of the last quarter and maximising the inherent diversity of our team.'

'Good. Good,' says Simon. He looks at you directly. He'd learned, at a recent training workshop, that a direct gaze is necessary to indicate engagement and connectivity. 'So, what are the measurable benchmarks that would indicate you'd consolidated the progress of the last quarter and maximised the diversity?'

God, measurable benchmarks.

'Well, even though we've lost three key performers,' (thanks to Lisa, you think to yourself), 'I'm on track to deliver the module on time and within budget.'

'Good, good,' says Simon. 'And what have I done to either assist or to hinder your performance?' His direct eye gaze is slipping. He doesn't want to look at you. The muscles around his mouth tighten.

You're tempted to say 'hinder' just to watch him arrange his face and attempt to look interested in your feedback.

'I feel very assisted, Simon,' you say.

His mouth relaxes. He smiles at you. 'Well, I certainly like to think I empower you to be the best you can be.'

Empowerment was one of The Hipster's favourite words. He would say, sadly, 'I'm just trying to empower you, Kat, to be your best self' – leading you to conclude that whoever your 'best self' was, it wasn't the current version of yourself.

'And I like to think that empowerment cascades down,' you say to Simon. 'I'm really working on not micromanaging my team.' This statement is performance-review gold. It shows that you care so much that you're all over the detail, treating the business like your own, but you're also aware of your own development needs around delegation.

Why couldn't you be this strategic with The Hipster? Why didn't you treat your relationship like a performance review? Meet those KPIs. Hit your Measurable Benchmarks.

Stay thin. Be interesting. Listen to his stories without interrupting and love his cat.

'Good, good,' Simon says, taking notes. His hands are small, and he wears a ring.

You wonder if his wife wears her ring or if her fingers are too swollen with the heat.

Focus, Kat. Ten more minutes and you're out of here.

'Do you have the tools and resources you need to perform your job?'

Resources and tools. Well, you need a flak jacket to get through the day with Lisa on the team. 'Yes, Simon, I feel well resourced.'

'Do you have any other concerns going forward?'

The phrase 'going forward' always strikes you as spectacularly redundant. You have some concerns going backwards. You had a good life until The Hipster left, and you hired Gollum Lisa.

You smile warmly. 'No, Simon, no other concerns.'

'What do you want your next position at this company to be?'

You want to be CEO. Stand behind that big desk, have long lunches in the boardroom and appear at Senate estimate hearings. Actually, maybe you don't.

'To be honest,' you say, 'I just see myself consolidating my current role before I progress anywhere.'

Nice. Humble but focused.

You glance at his list. He's been ticking things off. He's near the bottom. Good, no mention of complaints about Lisa and you should be out of here, home-free, in minutes.

'Okay, good, Kat. Also, just in relation to your FTEs, we are thinking of a change in relation to Lisa.'

Hell, and damnation. You look out the window. So close. You were so close to not having to admit your mistake in hiring her and your terror in managing her out. They're going to go over your head and manage her out themselves. This will look very bad for you.

You'll look weak, with poor judgement.

'Look, Simon,' you say, 'she was very good in the interview. To be honest, management should take some responsibility for this situation. If I hadn't been so under the pump maybe I'd have made a different hiring decision.' You lean forward. 'Just to let you know, she might become very difficult during the managing-out process.'

Simon looks confused. 'Managing her out? No, we're moving her into Julia's role.'

You feel like someone's belted you on the side of the head with a frypan. He must mean a different Lisa. Your brain loyally goes searching for another Lisa. It can only come up with Lisa Simpson.

'Lisa?' you say.

'Yes, Lisa Miles. We're moving Lisa into Julia's role.'

'Julia?' you say. Your brain goes searching. It can only come up with Julia Gillard. They're moving Lisa Simpson into Julia Gillard's role? Well, that'll never work. You stare out the window mouthing 'Julia Gillard'.

'Kat?' says Simon.

You must get a grip. This is an emergency. This is the worst idea anybody has ever had ever in the history of the world. The Lisa Simpson/Julia Gillard rumination has lost you critical strategic-planning time.

'Right, Simon, so Lisa into Julia's role,' you say, using the well-worn strategy of buying time by repeating what he has just said.

'Yes,' says Simon.

Lisa Miles, the fox in charge of the hen house.

'Simon, you're aware that part of Julia's role is client facing?'

'We're aware of that,' says Simon. 'We think Lisa has some really good people skills.'

Good people skills. Good god!

'Mm,' you say. 'She definitely has some great qualities.' Good strategy. Don't bag her out completely.

'Right,' says Simon.

'For instance, one of her really good qualities is her capacity to think outside the box,' you continue. 'She really gets into some blue-sky thinking.'

'Blue-sky thinking,' repeats Simon.

The repeat technique is getting some usage this afternoon.

'Now, the downside could be her tendency towards impetuosity.'

Oh, Kat, well done. You're on fire. Impetuosity, a word pulled from your nineteenth century literary vocabulary.

'Impetuous,' repeats Simon obediently. Though you observe he's stopped taking notes.

'Yes,' you say slowly, nodding as if giving it more consideration. 'So, Simon...'

'Before you go on, Kat, Lisa has mentioned there's been some...' he pauses, looking for the right term. 'Tension.'

The air has gone out of your body. You feel yourself to be a flat pack. Someone could take you home and turn you into a bookshelf. You are blindsided by the knowledge that Lisa has won. You are out of her league. She has usurped you. You put your hand up to your head.

Pull out a hair.

'Also, Lisa mentioned you might have been a bit stressed.'

You try to return the hair to your head. A bit stressed. Is this not Lisa's way of insinuating that you are unable to cope with life's usual ups and downs? That you're rendered useless in the face of a few challenges?

Your digestive system starts to respond to the unfolding disaster. An acrid, metallic taste appears in your mouth.

'So, just finally, Kat, in which area or areas would you like to improve?'

You swallow, then realise the metallic taste is the lens cleaner. You are now worried your breath smells like ethanol. He may have already concluded you've been drinking at work. Another indication of your out-of-control stress. Lisa probably planted the lens cleaner in your bag. She may even have switched the labels. Are there no lengths she won't go to, to bring you down?

'Kat, areas of improvement?'

Areas of improvement. Areas of improvement.

You'd like The Hipster to ring you and beg you to take him back. You'd like to be able to manage difficult people. You'd like to speak Chinese. You'd like to be less obsessional about The Hipster. You'd like to be less anxious. You'd like to drink less. You'd like to be interested in superannuation. You'd like to be vegan. You'd like to lose 2.75 kilos. You'd like to be less obsessional about your weight. You'd like to remember that every second Tuesday is glass recycling night. You'd like to be less of a pushover. You'd like to be tidier. You'd like to be less judgemental.

'Kat, Kat, are you okay?'

'Yes, I'm okay, Simon,' you say, attempting to smile. You feel the corners of your mouth go up, but your eye muscles remain resolutely immovable.

'That's good to know, though we do have support in the business if you feel the need to reach out.'

Normally the words 'reach out' irritate you intensely but as you look up at Simon, smiling at you, pen poised over your report, you feel your defensiveness wane. He seems to be genuinely concerned. You allow your gaze to rest briefly on the transplanted hairs clinging to his hairline. An image of him, standing on the sidelines of his local soccer game next to his steadfast wife, pushes itself past your judgement. There he is, pinioning his fringe against the wind, yelling support to his young son powering down the field. You see a man struggling with the notion of losing his masculinity.

You feel a rush of sympathy. You feel bad for judging him.

You'd like to have more courage.

You'd like to be less avoidant.

You'd like to be brave.

'Simon,' you say, 'we need to talk about Lisa.'

LET'S TALK ABOUT CORPORATE SPEAK, AND AVOIDANCE

Someone is putting their rubbish in your bin, causing it to overflow. You've seen them loading it in every Tuesday night. Do you:

a. Set your alarm for 3 am, go outside, take the offending garbage out and put it in someone else's bin? You know it's not ideal but well, you didn't start it.

b. Stop eating on Monday and Tuesday so there's less garbage? Also has side benefit of weight loss.

c. Hire a mafia hitman?

d. Calmly approach the person and ask them not to do it?

If you answered a, b or c, this chapter is for you. If you answered d, you are already perfect and may stop reading. Not really! You are likely kidding yourself and you're actually an undercover a, b or c.

Let's face it: avoidance as an option in difficult situations is very appealing. The downside is that invariably the avoided issue comes back to bite you.

As we've seen in earlier chapters, it's often the limbic system – the emotional part of our brain – that makes the decision to avoid something, and we then post-rationalise it in our frontal lobe. We're mostly unaware that this process is occurring. For example, if we don't go for a dental check-up because we're frightened of the pain, we might convince ourselves it's because we haven't got the time.

In the same way, Kat was aware she was being avoidant but felt it was justified. She didn't want to deal with the issue of Lisa, but also didn't want to confront what might happen if Lisa was as destructive as Kat believed. The result of the avoidance was costly. It was only when Kat saw through her initial perception of Simon, and understood he was being genuinely kind to her, that she decided to come clean and tell the truth.

What's that got to do with all the corporate speak?

Corporate speak is the ideal way to avoid confrontation – by saying something without really saying something. You can skirt around an issue, sounding competent, while biding your time until you exit the meeting and can go and get a coffee/wine/croissant. If you've worked in the corporate sector, you've probably attended a corporate event in which you were subjected to an hour and a half of relentless corporate speak. Nobody sets out to bore their audience to death and yet it's a frighteningly common occurrence. Using corporate speak is such a cultural norm that we can genuinely kid ourselves that we're effectively communicating.

We're just not. We've forgotten why we're speaking. It's not only to deliver information, but also to change or affect people's opinions. To do that, we need to use real language and not shy away from using emotion and personal stories. Yet we're so often guilty of leaning into the clinical familiarity of corporate speak. It's so ubiquitous, we don't even notice we're doing it when actually we're drowning in it.

Why does it matter? Because it's easy to use the phrase 'maximise inherent diversity', or a thousand others like it, without the speaker or the listener knowing precisely what is meant. And precision in speech is important. Without precision, it's possible to speak in a meaningful-*sounding* way without saying anything at all. Corporate language paints in such large, obscure strokes that nuance or specificity is impossible. And that allows everyone to remain unaccountable for outcomes, because no-one is quite sure what's being asked of them.

What happens to our personalities?

There is a general consensus in business that when we walk into the meeting, review, conference or boardroom, we take our personalities off – including our sense of humour – and leave them standing around on the corner smoking a cigarette until we're finished. No wonder they're grumpy on our return and demand to be given chips and a nice unwooded chardonnay.

The language of home, TV, books, children, theatre, happiness, tragedy, drunken nights out and cosy nights in – the language we use to describe our daily anguish to our friends on the phone – it's all abandoned as soon as we clock on and enter the realm of business.

If we really want to review someone's performance, and not just use the half hour as a box-ticking exercise, we need to ask genuine questions and encourage the other person to give considered answers.

One of the effects of clinical language is that it can keep the conversation sterile. This is an excellent way to avoid having to deal with anything difficult. Asking real questions, using real language and encouraging real answers mean that real issues and real emotion may arise during the meeting. This can be confronting for the manager, as dealing with complex issues needs emotional sensitivity and a deft touch. Managers should be assisted in developing the critical-thinking skills and emotional resilience to deal properly with their teams.

Loving yourself sounds like a tall order. Go for liking yourself most days.

Of course, the culture under which the business operates has a huge influence on whether conversations between managers and their people are real or not. But culture, and how we get it so wrong, is another book, people.

The availability heuristic again

Like Mrs Hume in chapter 3, Kat has made her assessment of Simon based on the availability heuristic. She draws conclusions about him based on examples that most easily come to mind. And the person who comes most easily to mind is Kat's Uncle Steve.

Thinking of examples that quickly come to mind is a time-efficient way to problem-solve. We're back relying on our prehistoric brains again. The availability heuristic is an evolutionary adaptation. Having to conjure everything from scratch would be a huge cognitive load.

The downside of heuristics is they allow for racism, sexism, ageism – in fact, any 'ism' – to arise. This results in us thinking of a person as part of a preconceived group rather than as an individual. Simon probably broadly shares the characteristics of Uncle Steve, so... how convenient, no further thinking required. He's like Uncle Steve, so she can play him like Uncle Steve.

Except she couldn't. Simon, although too reliant on corporate speak, did not allow himself to be diverted from the topic of Lisa, despite Kat's best efforts.

Getting smarter

Again, using critical thinking to approach issues is, well, critical. So, you need metacognition: thinking about your own thinking. You need to question your assumptions, query your biases and interrogate the veracity of your emotional reactions.

Kat catastrophised when confronted with the idea of Lisa's promotion. She allowed her limbic system to take over her brain, right when she needed her frontal lobe to increase her capacity for clear thinking.

The reason most of us don't genuinely question a person's interpretation of their reality is that our limbic systems are scared to death of conflict, so we wade around in corporate speak till the danger has passed.

We need a rebellion around corporate speak! It isn't just boring us to death, it's endangering us as a society. We can't track or challenge what's going on in our world if those who lead us use impenetrable language. Be brave and keep it real, people!

Get your thoughts straight

Mind Your Language

If you work in a corporate environment, and you are asked to give a presentation or conduct a performance review, make a note of how much corporate speak you've included. See what happens if you ask yourself, 'What do I actually mean by that sentence?' Strip out the corporate speak and use real language – language you'd use with friends. Note the different reaction you get from the person you're speaking to, or the audience.

Is the Sky Really Falling?

Do you catastrophise? If you have the propensity to assume the absolute worst, the first thing you have to do is notice that that's where your brain has gone. If you're a serial catastrophiser, you can use the Tame the Dragon technique from chapter 5 to distract your brain from its disastrous ruminations. If anxiety is an ongoing problem for you, go and see a registered psychologist.

Suspend Judgement

Are you having an intuitive response to someone, either in the positive or negative? This could be your brain layering on an old memory or perception. If you can, withhold judgement. Your perception may be accurate, but then again…

New Hire Halo

Is there someone in the media or your business that you trust because you like them in another context? For example, has someone come to your business with a halo from the business they worked in before? Has this skewed your thinking about their ideas and/or value to the business?

7

Kat goes to a party

You're going to a New Year's Eve party. Bethany from work has invited you. She drifts around the office with one raised eyebrow. She exhibits zero interest in office politics. You admire her enormously.

She's leaning on your desk, slowly swinging one leg. 'Come on, Kat,' she says. 'It's been six months since the dirtbag left you: you can't mope around forever. Come to my party. You might get lucky.'

Since The Hipster left you, people have been disturbingly forthcoming with their opinion of him.

'Okay,' you say. 'What shall I bring?'

'Scotch,' she says, wafting off.

So, the night of the party arrives. You're sitting outside a two-storey house with an unkempt lawn and a despondent-looking Christmas tree on the front verandah. You check your makeup in the rear-view mirror, once again questioning the need or appropriateness of green glitter eyeliner. The girl in the makeup section of David Jones had declared it very 'now', so you'd bought it. You look down at your red skirt and mentally go back over the five discarded outfits lying on your bed. Perhaps the green skirt was better. Also, it's unseasonably cold for December and you're wishing you'd brought a jacket. You're only fifteen minutes' drive away. You could go home, change, get a jacket and also possibly remove the eyeliner.

A tap at your window. It's Justine from HR. 'Hey Kat, you coming in?'

So, you're inside. You immediately feel overdressed. You should have worn jeans. But you'd vowed not to wear jeans until you'd lost the 2.75 five kilos. There's a woman in jeans who's bordering on a size fourteen. She's wearing thick blue glitter eyeliner and she's laughing loudly in an unconstrained way. She clearly belongs to a different species to you.

The house is packed with people you don't know. You stand uncertainly near the door.

You are saved by one of Bethany's housemates, who has just floated towards you draped in gold tinsel. Clearly, she's responsible for the denuding of the Christmas tree.

'Hey,' she says, proffering a tray of tofu on toothpicks. 'You have amazing hair. It's so Pre-Raphaelite.'

On this occasion you'd have to agree with her. It's the one thing about your appearance you actually like. 'Thanks,' you say.

'How do you know Bethy?' she says.

'I work in the same consulting firm.'

'Oh well.' She lays a commiserating hand on your arm.

'What do you do?' you ask, suspecting it will have something to do with yoga.

'I'm an intuitive healer.' She's still holding the tray under your nose. It smells like rancid nuts. 'Go on girl,' she says. 'They're vegan organic.'

You compliantly put one in your mouth. It tastes like a nutty kitchen sponge.

She reaches out, twists a lock of your hair around her finger. 'Are you sad?'

'Yes.'

She searches your eyes. 'I can feel the disturbance in you.'

'Oh,' you say.

'You're ungrounded,' she says. 'You need to walk barefoot on grass and watch your toxins and chemical intake while you're healing. I live a chemical-free life,' she says, tipping a bucket-sized vodka down her throat. 'You've gotta be Libran, right?'

'No,' you say. 'I'm not Libran.'

'Oh my god, I'm a Virgo. We love Librans. They're so empathic and intuitive.' She has clutched your wrist.

'No,' you say, shaking free of her grip. 'I said I'm not a Libran.' You are experiencing panic. Why did you agree to come to this party? You're trapped with a glittering drunk Vegan Virgo bearing a tray of impaled tofu.

She puts the tray on the floor and pulls a bell from her cavernous pockets, rings it at various points around your head. 'There is great healing in sound,' she pronounces. 'The vibrations will resonate with your sadness; allow it to be released.'

You stand compliantly until she rings the bell too close to your right ear and you pull away sharply.

'I can only do so much,' she says, like you'd booked a healing appointment and turned up with a bad attitude. She packs the bell away in her pocket.

'Right,' you say, trying to smile. 'I'm sorry.' You're worried she's going to report back to Bethany that you are arrogant. 'What's your name?' you ask the Vegan Virgo. 'My name's Kat.'

'Nat?'

'Kat.'

'Oh my god, I love that name. When I have a daughter, I'm definitely going to call her Natalie.'

Bethany approaches.

'I was just having a beautiful chat to your friend, Nat. I love Librans,' says the Vegan Virgo, as she wanders off into the crowd.

Bethany smiles benevolently at her retreating back. 'Hey, Kat, have you met my brother, Michael?'

Michael appears from behind her. A green shirt, the buttons done up wrong. Adult-sized teeth. A nose that looks like he's been in a fight and lost. Brown eyes. Brown hair. A trilby. He's wearing The Hipster's aftershave.

'Hey,' he says, his eyeline somewhere between your left shoulder and the front door. 'It's Kat, is it?'

'Yes, yes, it is.'

'I'll leave you two to it then,' says Bethany. She walks away, giving you a wink. This is clearly her paving the way for you to get lucky.

'So, how's things?' says Michael.

'Good. You?'

'Yeah, good.' He is unsmiling.

You wonder if Bethany has forced him talk to you. Your handbag is still over your shoulder. You produce the scotch. 'Like one?' you say.

'No thanks, I don't drink.'

'You don't drink at all?'

'No.'

'Oh, why?'

'I don't like the taste,' he says.

As if it's got anything to do with the taste, you think.

There is a pause. He points to the bottle of scotch. 'I can get you one of those if you like?' he offers.

Why did Bethany ask you to bring scotch? It's embarrassing. It's the drink of choice of your father. An old man's drink. You should have bought vermouth, inferring martinis.

'It's okay, I don't actually drink scotch.'

'Did you bring the bottle for someone else?'

'Um. No.'

There is another pause.

'Your skirt's nice.' His mother has clearly told him to pay women a compliment upon meeting them.

'Thanks,' you say. 'I was going to wear a green skirt but decided on the red.'

Oh god, you think, why do people have parties?

There is a third pause. You both look around the room, searching for conversation impetus.

Someone turns the music up. People start dancing.

'Shall we join them?' he says.

The size fourteen jeans woman dances alone with abandon. You admire her enormously.

The last time you danced was at the blue light disco in Year Seven.

'No, I'm good.' You look down, note the trouser legs of his jeans are tucked into his socks. 'You ride your bike here?' you say, pointing to his right leg.

'No,' he says, 'why?'

'Oh, I just noticed your jeans tucked into your socks and I assumed...'

He looks down at his right leg and pulls the hem out, leaving his left trouser leg tucked into his sock. 'No,' he says. 'No bike.'

'Right. I just thought...'

You both stand there looking at his feet.

The Vegan Virgo reappears. She must have been having a good go at the chemical-free vodka because she's now very drunk. 'Hi, my little Libran friend,' she says.

'I'm not actually a Libran,' you say.

She narrows her eyes suspiciously at you. 'You sure?'

'Yes, I'm sure. Excuse me, I'm going to get myself a martini.'

'Typical Libran,' you hear her say as you walk off.

You glance back. They are both looking at you, united in their disapproval.

By the time you get to the other side of the room, she has pulled the bell out of her pocket and is ringing it near Michael's head. He is standing there, smiling at her and nodding appreciatively.

You should have done that. Would it have really hurt you just to listen to the bell and pretend you're a Libran? She'll ask Bethany why she invited such an obnoxious friend. You've offended everyone you've had a conversation with, which, admittedly, is just two people, but still. Michael and the Vegan Virgo are probably discussing your ungrounded social skills right now.

You don't care. You want to go home. You dislike everyone at this party.

You skirt the edge of the room, head to the kitchen and grab a beer from the fridge, wondering to yourself why you had to mention a martini.

You head upstairs to Bethany's oasis of a bathroom. You walk in, shut the door. The bathroom is one of those fifties relics. Accidental retro cool. All pink tiles. You're quite buoyed by the look of yourself in the bathroom mirror. The pink tiles are bouncing off your skin, making you look positively dewy. Until you turn on the plug-in lights with the magnifier.

The bathroom is transformed into an operating theatre. You wouldn't have been out of place wearing scrubs. Dewy-you disappears. Your skin is appalling. Your pores look like moon craters. Your face under the scrutiny of the magnifier is deeply distressing.

You sit on the bath rim researching 'laser resurfacing' on your phone. You're unimpressed by the before-and-after shots. If you're going to resurface your skin, you'll need a beauty therapist willing to use a belt sander.

You become aware of knocking on the bathroom door. You must have been in there for at least twenty minutes by the looks of your search history. You shut your phone, walk to the door and open it. Rebecca from The Real Estate is standing there. Looking amazing. Thinner than when you last saw her. Fifty-six kilos. Possibly fifty-five. She's probably adhering to The Hipster's vegan diet. No sneaking to the fridge for late-night gorging of real cheese and glasses of planet-destroying cow's milk.

'Hi!' you say brightly.

'Hi, Kat,' she says coolly. She is standing in the hall under the flattering light of a dim 40-watt globe. Her skin looks luminous.

You are standing under the bathroom light. You put your hand to your own moon-crater face. 'So, how are you?' you say, like she's a favoured work colleague who's been away with appendicitis and has just returned.

'I'm good, thanks,' she answers, giving you a thin smile.

There is a silence while you both stand there looking at each other.

'Do you mind?' She indicates her desire to enter the bathroom. You are blocking the door.

'Sure, yeah sorry.' You step out, she steps in and closes the door.

She's probably wondering how The Hipster stayed with you for so long, with your bad social skills and hideous skin.

This party is a Disaster. You don't care if you've only been here for an hour and fifteen. You're going home.

You head down the hallway, feeling for your keys in your bag, when the sound of a voice in the stairwell stops you in your tracks.

'My circadian rhythm is absolutely in sync,' the voice says. 'I haven't used an alarm clock in years. I set the clock in my brain and, ping! I'm awake.'

It's The Hipster.

You flatten yourself against the wall like a spy. You have to get out. However, you can't resist having a look. You go to the bannister. Look over.

Your heart turns over. The Hipster's standing on the stairs smiling down at someone. Must be a female. That smile is reserved for females. He's wearing the jeans you really like and his favourite Schrödinger's Cat t-shirt, which says, 'Wanted Dead and Alive.'

You withdraw back to the hallway, wait for your heart to settle down. The bathroom door is still shut. Rebecca from The Real Estate may also be realising her skin is not as perfect as other mirrors had led her to believe.

The Hipster has lowered his voice to a soft murmur, but you recognise the intimate tone. A female giggle in response.

You move back to the bannister, chance another look.

The beneficiary of his smile is now standing on the step below him. Of course, it's the Vegan Virgo. She's manoeuvring tofu past his tiny teeth, into his mouth. The Vegan Virgo is perfect for him. She wouldn't touch cheese if her life depended on it.

You observe the look he's giving her. That tilt of the head intimates that she is the most important person in the room.

You feel your heart squeeze. If only he would look at you like that again.

You look back over your shoulder. The bathroom door handle is turning. Rebecca from The Real Estate is coming out and will see you spying over the bannister. You're trapped. Going downstairs is impossible.

You launch yourself down the hallway and open the first door. You're in Bethany's bedroom. As is her dog. A silver Great Dane on her bed. It opens one eye and lifts its head off the pillow, growls softly. Looks at you.

You are unfamiliar with big dogs. You don't know if you should look back at it or look away. You remember Mrs Hume saying that you shouldn't look a dog in the eye, as it will take it as a sign of aggression. You decide stillness and averting your gaze is the best strategy. Averting your gaze takes your eyeline out onto Bethany's balcony.

A balcony. A first-floor balcony. You've seen people in movies escape from sticky situations by climbing over balconies. You're in a sticky situation. Maybe you can lower yourself from the balcony and avoid contact with all current inhabitants of the house.

You risk a direct look at the dog. It seems uninterested, but what if you're misreading the signals, and it's just biding its time before it launches itself off the bed and pins you to the floor with its great paws, slobbering and growling in your face? Bethany, alerted by the growling, will come running in with The Hipster, Rebecca from The Real Estate and the Vegan Virgo in tow. The Vegan Virgo will try to calm you down by dropping homeopathic rescue remedy drops into your mouth. Your life will be over.

So far so good, though. You make your way in a casual manner across the room to the balcony door. You feel the dog's gaze, following your progress.

You get to the door, open it, go across the balcony and look down. There are bins haphazardly arranged below. Mrs Hume would be aghast. You should be able to go over the balcony and gain a foothold on one of them. You look back at the dog. It's still looking over its shoulder at you. If you could just make it from the balcony to the ground without breaking a leg, your problems would be over.

You hear Rebecca from The Real Estate's voice in the hallway. You are galvanised into action. You sling your bag over your shoulder, go to the edge of the balcony, look down to the ground, ignore the wave of vertigo and sling one leg over.

You are now straddling the railing, one leg out and one in. The dog is still lying like an inscrutable emperor on the bed.

You sling the other leg over. It's cold. You're now poised on the narrow ledge on the outer side of the balcony, looking down at the bins. You glance back into the room. The dog has moved off the bed and is standing at the doorway to the balcony. It's enormous: about the size of a small horse.

You look down again, grab hold of the railing and lower your right leg. It makes tenuous contact with the recycle bin. Your head is now level with the floor of the balcony.

You hear the door to the bedroom open. You look up. The dog must have stealth-crawled across the balcony, because it's now three centimetres away from you. You can see the flecks in its eyes and feel its hot breath.

'Who's a pretty boy,' you say, like he's a parrot.

The sound of advancing footsteps across the wooden floor.

'You okay there, boy? What you looking at? Why's the door open? It's cold.'

Michael appears behind the dog. Looks over the railing. 'Kat?'

'Hey, Michael.'

'Front door not your thing?'

'No, I'm more a balcony girl.'

'Right. You want to come back over?'

'No, I'm good.'

'If you move your left leg twenty centimetres to the right, you'll connect with the bin,' he says.

You do so. You're now standing on tiptoes on the recycler.

There's a long pause, in which your fingers start to ache.

'Your sister's dog is big,' you say.

'Yes.' He scratches behind the dog's left ear. 'You're a big boy, aren't you, Dave?' he says.

'I have a cat. It's my ex's,' you say.

'Right.'

'He's in your sister's lounge room. My ex, not the cat,' you add.

'Right.'

'Anyway, I'll be off,' you say.

He crouches down and takes hold of your hands through the bars.

You lower yourself thirty centimetres, until you're standing squarely on the bin.

He releases your hands.

You crouch low on the bin, feeling it wobble under your weight. If you'd lost that 2.75 kilos it wouldn't have been a problem. You jump and land successfully on the grass.

'I'm going to put a reminder in my phone,' he calls down to you. 'Untuck pants from socks.'

'Okay,' you say. You look back up at him leaning over the balcony.

Ninja dog is still staring silently at you.

'Typical Capricorn,' you call up. 'Good social skills but has issues with socks.' You imagine him smiling in the dark.

You start across the lawn and are halfway to freedom, when the front door opens and an oblong of light spills onto the grass. You leap to the perimeter. The Hipster's voice, carried on the back of his outrage, reaches you as you sprint across the rest of the lawn and out onto the street.

'You're being ridiculous, I was just talking to her,' he is saying.

You reach the car, fling open the door, throw your handbag and yourself into it, and lock the door. You sit, one hand on your beating heart, and look back at the house in the rear-view mirror. The oblong of light, The Hipster and his outrage have been reabsorbed back into the house.

Rebecca from The Real Estate had better be careful. The Hipster doesn't like being questioned.

You sit in the quiet sanctity of your car, safe in the knowledge that whatever dramas are currently being played out in the house of horrors, they're no longer on you. You sit on your hands and think about Michael's hands on yours – how they'd felt lived-in. And it's while you're sitting in the car, waiting for your heartbeat to slow, that your brain begins running the tape of the party. As you watch it, an image keeps flickering at the edge of the screen – indistinct but insistent. You spool the tape back and watch it carefully, and there it is, camouflaged amid the general jungle of deception. A casual lie. Small but significant.

The story The Hipster had told about not needing an alarm clock, because he could set the clock in his brain, was false. You'd had to shake him awake every morning. It was like trying to raise the dead. His circadian rhythm story was a lie.

It's as you start the car that you realise: he is a Liar. A cheat, and a Liar.

THE SPOTLIGHT EFFECT

Do you have difficulty navigating your way through complex social situations, or do you glide through them like a hot knife through butter?

Try this quick quiz.

You have been invited to a work networking event. Do you:

a. Take three weeks to organise an outfit, arrive, talk to your friend from across the office for an hour, get an Uber home and watch Netflix?

b. Arrive, drink too much, drape your arm around the CEO and tell her this is the best job you've ever had, then resign the next day?

c. Take three weeks to organise an outfit, then stay home and watch Netflix?

d. Play your usual role of effortless socialite? You totally nail all social situations. Social events are your place to shine. People who watch Netflix on their own are losers.

Okay, d, I'll leave you with your extroverted charm and talk to a, b, and c!

Remember: we have tribal brains, so fitting in is all-important

Parties and other social gatherings, including work events, are fraught experiences for so many of us – it's a wonder we put ourselves through them.

One of the reasons we do is that we're tribal. As in chapter 3, when Mrs Hume made assumptions about her neighbours based on their ethnicity, a social setting is another context in which the tribal part of our brains is activated. We are biologically hardwired to socialise with others, so our brains are highly sensitive to being an outsider – no matter what context the tribe exists in.

A family is a tribe. A football team is a tribe. A group of friends is a tribe. A religion is a tribe. An organisation is a tribe. A group of people at a party standing in a circle may have only met ten minutes ago but, if we're standing on the outside of it, they look like a tribe to our brain.

We may dress up in nice dresses and carry large handbags, but underneath it all we are first and foremost social animals. Being social animals, feeling the need to belong can bring with it a large dose of fear that we *don't* belong.

So maybe you haven't faced off a Great Dane and climbed over a balcony to escape an encounter with an ex, but you've undoubtedly had some deeply uncomfortable experiences at networking events, parties and speaking up in meetings.

Kat's fight-flight-freeze was triggered

So, why would Kat go to such extreme measures to escape an uncomfortable situation, climbing over a balcony? Well, her anxiety reached such a peak that her fight-flight-freeze response kicked in and her limbic system was pushed into 'flight'.

Remember in chapter 5, when Kat was too frightened to jump into the skipping rope and speak up at the meeting? Similarly, in the context of the party, her brain perceived her to be in danger, so released a cascade of chemicals that hijacked her thinking, and seriously affected her decision-making. And not in a good way.

The spotlight effect – is everybody really looking at you?

Kat's entire experience was marred by self-consciousness. She was worried about people's reactions to her clothing and glitter eyeliner. She was also embarrassed about the scotch and was amazed that a woman she perceived to be overweight would dance in public when Kat herself wouldn't dance at all. She also thought people were still talking about her after she'd left them.

What caused this perception that whatever she did, people looked at and assessed her? Well, it's called the spotlight effect. First coined by psychologists Thomas Gilovich and Kenneth Savitsky,[7] the spotlight effect is that feeling you get when someone is clearly in a bad mood and you immediately assume it's because of you; or when you walk into a room and people seem to go quiet, and you assume it's because they were talking about you. There are a thousand topics that people could be discussing, and a thousand reasons why someone is in a bad mood, yet we're so quick to decide it's because of us.

We think people are looking at us more than they are.

The reason the spotlight effect is so pervasive is that we are exquisitely aware of our feelings and thoughts. If you're a sensitive person, every emotional ripple can feel like a thunderous wave, so it seems impossible that other people aren't aware of this, too. So, if there's tension in a room you've just walked into, you think it's probably something to do with you.

---

7   Gilovich, T, Medvec, VH & Savitsky, K (2000), 'The spotlight effect in social judgment: An egocentric bias in estimates of the salience of one's own actions and appearance', *Journal of Personality and Social Psychology*, vol. 78, no. 2, pp. 211–222.

None of the thoughts that Kat ascribed to other people would have been accurate. The truth is, we have no idea what other people are thinking – but we can safely assume that we wildly overestimate the degree to which we're at the centre of others' cognitive processes. Kat's general perception of how she was perceived and judged, for everything from the minutiae of her appearance to the slightest interactions, was amplified. Michael and the Vegan Virgo were not discussing Kat's ungrounded social skills. In fact, I happen to know they were talking about solving the Middle East conflict. This is how confirmation bias dovetails nicely with the spotlight effect. Kat assumed they were talking about her as confirmation that she was socially awkward.

The spotlight effect is a large contributor to social anxiety, leading us to believe that everybody is talking/looking at/judging us. It's a big reason why we spend so much time worrying about what other people think, and why we believe people focus on us much more than they actually do.

Your perception is worth questioning. You may very well be wrong. It's helpful to remember that everybody is hyper-involved in their own thinking and feelings. They're much too self-involved to be worried about you.

You don't have to be nice all the time

Kat's response to this skewed perception – that everybody is looking at her/judging her – is to ensure that at all times she's being 'nice' and doesn't do anything that could invite unwanted negative attention (like dancing). This is not everybody's response to self-consciousness. Some people may become withdrawn or aggressive but, for the purposes of this story, we'll stick with Kat's response, which is to be nice.

This compulsion to be nice, to always be easy, compliant, agreeable and pleasant, needs some analysis. If you're highly driven to be likeable, it means you'll find yourself in situations where you'd like to push back, and you won't. You'd like to say, 'No, I don't want to do that,' but you'll be disinclined to do so in case you offend someone. You'll interpret holding your ground as being difficult.

There were a number of things Kat could've done differently if she hadn't been under the thrall of the spotlight effect and wasn't so driven to be nice. She could have:

- said to the Vegan Virgo, 'I don't want you to ring your bell near my head, and no thanks – I don't like tofu.'
- brought along a drink she liked, instead of going with Bethany's casual suggestion of scotch
- danced with abandon
- had a quick look in the bathroom mirror, then moved on – instead of formulating a new plan to combat her moon-crater face
- been less avoidant of Rebecca from the Real Estate and The Hipster. This might have engendered a sense of autonomy in her
- laughed off her gaffe about Michael's socks
- restricted herself to two choices of clothing, instead of spending hours trying to find the perfect outfit
- exited through the front door.

The woman in the jeans with the glitter eyeliner, and perfectionism

Kat was amazed that somebody who wasn't rake thin would wear jeans and dance and laugh. The woman in jeans is emblematic of someone who's comfortable in their own skin. Either that, or she had a few martinis under her belt.

Author's note: I'm not advocating getting drunk as a way to ameliorate social anxiety. Though it's interesting to note how many people use alcohol to intervene in the brain's processing and dampen down the social fear response.

Who knows what life journey the woman in jeans had experienced? Maybe she'd always been comfortable in herself? Maybe she'd had to reason her way out of a perfectionistic notion of the way she should look and behave? Whatever her history, she was comfortable with who she was and that is the ultimate aim.

Getting smarter

The whole social experience is fraught. However, it's really helpful to remember that we don't have any idea what's going on inside other people's heads. It's easy to endow other people with confidence that they may not feel. If you think about yourself for a second, how often is the way you behave opposite to how you're feeling? It's true that some people are more adept at moving gracefully through social situations than others, but a large proportion of people appear relaxed when actually they're not.

Our brains can be highly attuned to social rejection, so, instead of giving yourself a hard time about being socially nervous, understand what's behind the fear, and start to gently challenge some of your perceptions. Berating yourself for having 'stupid thoughts' is unhelpful. Your brain is primed to try to fit in and worries if it perceives it's not. Understand that you're trying to live up to arbitrary, impossible standards, set by an archaic, anxious part of your brain, and give yourself a break.

Get your thoughts straight

It's Not About You

If you walk into a room and you sense a negative atmosphere, or someone ignores you, it's probably not about you. Go about your business.

Dance like No-one's Watching

People aren't evaluating if your jeans are too tight. They're also not looking at your dance style. Get up. Shake that booty.

Loosen the Corset (Again)

If you're triple-guessing yourself before you open your mouth in a social setting, trying to find the perfect thing to say, try asking a question. People love talking about themselves.

Nice as Pie

Watch out for making decisions based on ensuring you will be approved of or liked. You will never be universally liked, and that's okay.

8

Kat pitches an idea

You're at the Roadshow. David Firth, the CEO, has just taken the stage. Last week, you were alone in the lift with him for three agonising floors. You'd tried to recall the elevator pitch you'd been encouraged to develop by a communications consultant, but you couldn't even remember the opening line. So, you'd stood perfectly still, staring fixedly at the door – hoping he wouldn't notice you were there.

He'd noticed.

'So, how are the numbers today? And, more importantly, how are you?'

To which you'd answered, 'The numbers and me is well... are well, thank you, Mr Firth.'

He'd said, 'Great news. Call me David. And what's your name?'

'Kat Mitchell, sir.'

Sir? Oh god, you'd thought, what was wrong with you? You'd come over all Oliver Twist. You may as well have curtsied.

He'd been immaculately turned out, with a nod to Silicon Valley. Good-looking, with really good teeth.

It's the same today. He's leaning languidly on the lectern while channelling the engagement style of *Q&A*'s Hamish Macdonald.

'Each one of you in this room,' he's saying, 'is an ideas generator. An innovation ideator.'

That's me, you think. I'm an ideas ideator.

You weren't much of an ideas ideator, however, during the networking event prior to the Roadshow.

Who invented networking? What possible benefit was there to forcing people to stand in a room with a cup and saucer in one hand and a mini muffin in the other, talking to people they'd only ever nodded to over a desk divider? And also, what was the point of the saucer? How did it assist in managing the liquid in the cup?

Saucers, you think, are a nod to a more genteel period. If you're utilising a saucer, you should be sitting in a drawing room with a lace collar, balancing the teacup atop the saucer while saying, 'Yes, Mr Grainger, I agree entirely: the hedge is too high.' Not making use of the saucer as a final resting place for the muffin case.

You'd stood to the side of the room wondering what to do about your sticky fingers when you'd noted Rosemary from HR – whom you knew fairly well – talking to two people unfamiliar to you. Breaking into a group is always agonising, and they were already deep in conversation, so you'd mentally tossed about a few opening statements, finally landing on, 'Morning everyone. You're doing better with the muffins than I am.'

This opening statement proved to be a success, as the woman to the left of Rosemary had turned to you, offering you a wipe from her bag. 'I won't need it,' she said, 'No muffins for me, I've been gluten-free low-carb for thirteen days.'

'Do you know Odette from Risk?' said Rosemary. 'She carries her entire life in her handbag.'

As you were rubbing your hands with Odette's wipe, your phone had beeped in your pocket. It was Dan from Compliance, complaining that he couldn't hold your seat for much longer.

So, now you are in the conference centre, three rows from the front, sitting next to Dan from Compliance, still clutching Odette's wipe. Behind the CEO, an opening video is being shown. A smiling Alice from Customer Service is delighting her customer by pointing to a graph on her computer.

'Yeah right,' says Dan from Compliance. 'Alice just lives every day for her customers.'

You don't find Dan particularly compliant.

He swivels and turns to the back of the room. 'Hope there are some mini quiches left.'

The video fades and the CEO resumes his presentation. 'When I started in this company, I worked in the mail room. I guess it would be called the email room now.'

We all laugh dutifully. Dan from Compliance snorts.

'I was young but curious,' the CEO continues. 'I worked my way up in this company by asking questions. Not just asking questions, but listening to the answers. The years passed and I kept asking questions.'

He leans forward. Dangles his hands over the front of the lectern.

'One of our major operating principles was developed from a conversation I had with a junior marketer I ran into at the coffee shop on level twenty-two.'

He stands up straight, holds onto the sides of the lectern. 'I say to each of you: don't sit on the sidelines and wait for permission.'

He's morphing from Hamish Macdonald into an evangelical preacher. 'Be the person who allows their thinking to expand outside the confines of what we already know.'

He moves out from behind the lectern and jumps down into the audience, brandishing his handheld mike. 'Be the person who tears up the rule book and writes their own.' His voice rises to fever pitch. 'Be the person who believes in themselves.' His voice suddenly drops. 'Be the person who has an idea and says, "I'm taking this to David. Right now. Here, today".'

You wonder if he's married. The Hipster was in his thirties, which was probably the problem. Too young. The CEO is probably in his late forties. Likely divorced. Maybe ready for a second family. You'd be good at blended families. You could have children of your own and be quite comfortable ferrying your stepchildren to soccer and attending academic excellence awards nights. You are the sort of person who doesn't need to be genetically related to form attachment.

Look at you and The Cat.

The CEO seems spent from his oratory. He moves slowly back up to the lectern and steeples his hands under his chin. 'Now, employee wellness is a key plank in our talent engagement and retention strategy. We're running daily yoga classes and mindfulness training, free for all employees. Do take advantage of these because, as we know, stress management is key to performance.'

You'd like to tell him that yoga and mindfulness didn't improve The Hipster's performance.

Dan from Compliance has been on Facebook this entire time. He turns to you, rolls his eyes.

'Yeah right, downward-facing frigging dog in my lunch break.'

You're with Dan.

The CEO continues. 'Now, you have two weeks before the end of the financial year to get your ideas to me – and remember, small ideas can be game changers.' He pauses. 'Tanya, stand up.'

A rotund woman in a snake-print dress stands at her chair, looks around the room and smiles warmly.

'Tanya is my executive assistant. Now, I know she looks scary, but she actually doesn't bite.'

We all laugh too hard.

'So,' he concludes, seemingly looking directly at you. 'If you have an idea, you come up to the twenty-eighth floor and say to her, "I need to speak to David." She knows you're my priority.'

'I know it's a cliché, but my door is always open.'

Cut forward four days and you're standing in front of friendly Tanya's desk, which is like an island in the middle of the massive, virtually empty floor. You've been given permission by the CEO to circumvent the protocols. You're breathless with excitement. For too long you've been treading water with your life. There has to be more than Netflix and The Cat. You hold a document in your hand. It details an amazing idea that's going to catapult your career and cement your reputation as an innovation exemplar. You'd mooted it before in a working-group meeting, but it was too visionary for the troglodytes sitting around the table. But you know it's a winner, and time is of the essence.

One wall is a long window overlooking Sydney Harbour. Two walls are the repository for a McCubbin, a Nolan and a Modern. The CEO himself must be secreted somewhere behind the fourth wall, though there is no discernible door.

Tanya, in a leopard-print dress, is tapping away at her computer.

You'll probably win Australian Businesswoman of the Year. Then you can have your own busy executive assistant in a leopard-print dress. You'll have lost the 2.75 kilos, so you'll look great on the podium. The Hipster will offer to give interviews to the newspapers. You'll tell the papers you've never heard of him, before you forgive and marry him.

Tanya is still tapping on her computer.

You stand there looking avidly around the vast area as if your purpose is to take in the artwork.

Eventually she looks up. She is not smiling warmly. 'Yes?'

'Oh, hi,' you say, as if you're surprised by her presence.

She looks at you.

You gesture towards the window. 'Great view. I'm Kat Mitchell.'

She continues to look at you.

'Um, I was wondering if I could see David?'

'David Firth?'

No, David of David and Goliath. 'Yes, David Firth.'

'Do you have an appointment?' She knows you don't.

'Um, no, but I do have an idea.'

'An idea?'

'Yes, a proposal around data mining.'

'Right. Mr Firth has back-to-back meetings.'

The balloon of excitement in your chest starts to deflate. 'Right,' you smile engagingly. 'It wouldn't take up much of his time.'

She pauses. 'So Legal and Risk have signed off?' She knows they haven't.

'Well, I thought I'd run it past him first.'

'Once you've been through Legal, Risk, Finance and IT, get back to me and I'll endeavour to find you an appointment to see Mr Firth.'

You keep standing there. But Mr Firth said you didn't bite, and his door was always open, you want to say.

She has gone back to her computer. You hold your position. You imagine yourself running past her, bursting into his office, handing him the document, him reading it while doing a one-buttock lean on his desk, then smiling up at you, amazed, and saying, 'This has got legs.'

You look past Tanya at the walls. With no discernible door, there's just smooth, impenetrable wall as far as the eye can see. What if you ran towards what you thought was his office and were stuck there clawing at the wall?

At that moment, Tanya catapults herself out of her chair, grabs some papers and, in a blur of leopard print, sprints across the floor.

She must utter some incantation, as a portion of the wall opens and reveals the CEO inside. As she arrives at his desk, he stands up, reaches for the document Tanya's proffering, and answers his phone at the same time. Tanya virtually genuflects as she hands him the documents. He flicks through the documents while Tanya stands before him, her head down, her hands clasped in front of her like a schoolgirl caught smoking and sent to the headmaster's office. He finishes his flicking. He hangs up his phone, sits down and waves the document in Tanya's direction.

'Tanya, this was meant to go yesterday. That was the Minister's office. You've been really disorganised lately. You're going to have to get your act together.'

'I'm so sorry,' she says. 'But I did send this version to you yesterday, and you said you wanted to check it before I forwarded it to the Minister.' She starts wringing her hands.

'You're blaming me?' he says, rising.

'No, not at all, I just—'

'I've just had the Minister's Chief of Staff talking to me in a very terse manner,' he says. 'Where's your discretionary energy in these matters? It's one of our cultural characteristics.'

She turns towards the door. You can see her face. It's a picture of misery and apology.

This is maybe not the time to push your ideas ideator concept.

The door that's always open is now slowly shutting.

'Okay, well, thanks, Tanya,' you call out into the dwindling gap. 'I'll just get this innovative ideation idea signed off, I'll start with Legal and I'll be back really soon.' You're waving like you're on a train station, and Tanya and the CEO are off on a holiday to Brighton.

You scurry to the lift. Get in and push the button for Legal's floor.

Craig from Legal is sitting at his desk, drinking a coffee. He is wearing heavy-rimmed black glasses, making him look like he's wandered out of the optometrist mid eye exam.

You explain to him that you need someone to look over the document for you.

'Okay,' says Craig. 'What is it?'

'It's an idea around data mining. I'm hauling it around to get costings.'

Leafing through the document, he looks up at you. 'Okay, you're working with Quinn?'

'Quinn?' you say.

'Yeah, Quinn O'Reilly from Risk.'

'No, why?' you ask.

'Well, he ran this past Anthony yesterday.'

Your scalp begins to prickle with sweat. You remember back to the meeting when you'd presented the idea. There, sitting opposite you, was the loathsome Quinn O'Reilly, staring off into the distance. He'd voted it down. The filthy idea stealer.

'You'll find there are variations.'

He's still flicking through it. 'No, it seems pretty much the same.'

'Okay,' you say. 'Well, I'm going to need sign-off. Quinn and I aren't working on this together.'

'Oh, okay,' says Craig. 'Well, does Quinn know you're hawking his idea around?'

Your scalp tightens, and the beginnings of a headache tug at your temples. You want to kick him. 'It's actually my idea, and I need to get sign-off.'

'It's going to be tricky getting into Anthony's diary.'

'Well, I see Quinn got into Anthony's diary.'

'Well, you know Quinn,' he says. 'He knows everyone.'

You do know Quinn. He sits like a giant gecko conducting his meetings in the cafe downstairs, trapping acquaintances with his long tongue as they pass. He's the king of syndicating. You can hear his thick Irish brogue cannoning across the foyer. Australians are complete suckers for a Celtic cliché. You've actually heard him say, 'Top of the morning to ya.'

'Craig,' you say, 'I would really appreciate the opportunity to get into Anthony's diary. Really, really soon.'

'I'll do what I can,' says Craig. 'But he's only got so many hours in the day.'

You've got sweat dripping down the back of your neck. The biggest opportunity of your lifetime is going to be swiped from under your nose. The Businesswoman of the Year and podium are rapidly receding. The loathsome Irish Gecko is going to get there first.

Opportunist.

You put both hands on Craig's desk and lean across in a menacing manner. 'I'll be back this afternoon, Craig. I expect to be able to have a meeting with Anthony.'

You walk away from his desk, without looking back. This is difficult, as the lift is taking a long time and his desk is right near it. Still, you stare resolutely ahead. You feel a soft tug on your arm. You turn.

It's Craig. 'Your mum texted. Pip is getting married,' he says, handing you your phone, which you'd left on his desk.

That'd be right. Every single female in your family is choosing this year to get married. Pip is marrying a hedge fund broker at twenty-six. The wedding will probably be in New Zealand. You'll be expected to fork out for the plane fare, share a room at the Hilton with your parents, and contribute to solid silver candlesticks selected from the David Jones wedding register. When you marry, you'll insist on getting married in somebody's garden and no gifts unless anybody is attached to giving you one thousand thread count Egyptian cotton sheets. Simple off white is fine. The Cat can be the ring bearer. You can attach the ring to her collar. This could be awkward if The Hipster is not the groom, but The Cat is nothing if not adaptable.

The lift doors open and there stands Quinn, talking animatedly to Anthony.

You step into the lift. Here's your moment, Kat. You're in an elevator. Use your elevator pitch to reclaim your idea and get Anthony to sign it off. You've probably only got three floors.

But Quinn's arm is holding the door. He acknowledges you with a friendly smile as Anthony steps around you.

'But that sounds terrific, Quinn. So, tee off at, say, seven-thirty?' says Anthony.

Why didn't you take up golf, Kat? Executives play golf. Anthony's not going to be interested in hopping on the Pilates reformer at 7.30 a.m.

And they're out of the lift. You watch their retreating backs as the doors close.

In a welter of indecision, you call out. 'Excuse me, Anthony!' But they've gone.

The CEO had inferred that pitching an idea to him was a matter of wandering up to the thirty-fifth floor with your document, where Tanya, his friendly executive assistant, would facilitate your easy access into his office. In your imaginings, after she'd seen you comfortably seated at his desk, she'd said, 'Ms Mitchell, can I get you a coffee or a juice?' When you'd declined, she'd smilingly left the office, closing the door behind her so you and the CEO could discuss your brilliant idea in a mature, considered manner.

So far, the process has been like being in a non-English-speaking country and finding your passport has expired ten minutes before you get on your flight.

You lean against the mirrored wall of the lift and punch the floor number for Risk with the toe of your shoe.

The lift doors open to reveal Odette from the networking session from last week.

She's sitting at her desk, working at a mindfulness colouring book.

'Hey Odette, how are you?'

She looks up briefly. 'Good, thanks.'

'It's me, Kat. I met you at last week's networking session. You kindly gave me a wipe.'

'Oh, yes!' She smiles up at you. 'I'm still gluten-free, low-carb. Seventeen days.'

You return the smile. 'Wow, well done! Well, can you run an eye over this proposal? I need sign-off ASAP.'

Her smile fades. 'I'm actually on a break, Kat.' So much for the relationship-building at the network session.

She's busy colouring a Labrador puppy blue. She sees you looking at it. 'I let my imagination go. It's healthy and stress-reducing.'

'Right,' you say, like she's seven. 'It looks great. So, when you've finished your break, can you run an eye over this?'

'No can do. I'm in Jenny's role. She's gone on mat leave. You know she'd been trying IVF for nine years, then stopped it and fell pregnant within a year. How's that?'

You don't know Jenny, and discussion of pregnancies makes you feel inadequate.

'Amazing,' you say. 'So who's in your role?'

'Helen.'

You hand her the proposal. 'Could you have Helen run an eye over this, please?'

She flicks through it. 'Oh, right. No need. Helen signed off on this yesterday. For Quinn.'

Your stomach lurches. 'When did she receive it?'

'Yesterday.'

'She received it and signed off on the same day? That's some turnaround,' you say.

'Yeah, all good,' she says.

She turns her attention to the puppy's ears.

'Anyway, it's not the same proposal. I need to talk to Helen.'

She calls over your shoulder across the desks. 'Hey Tamzin, where's Helen?'

'Not here,' calls Tamzin.

'When will she be back?' you call to Tamzin.

'Hang on,' she replies. 'I'll check with Hamish.'

Tamzin picks up the phone. 'Hamish,' she says, 'where's Helen?'

There is a pause.

'Oh right, oh no, yeah, no.' She puts her hand over the phone. 'He says Helen's off today. Her dog died.'

Odette pauses her colouring in. 'Oh, that's so sad,' she says. 'I love dogs.'

Quinn will be returning triumphant to the CEO's office, having got sign-off, while you stand here dealing with dead dogs and Odette and her colouring-in book.

Tamzin continues. 'We lost Barry a year ago. It's like it was yesterday.'

Why have people adopted the habit of calling dogs by human names, like Dave? The next-door neighbour's Spoodle is called Howard. She's forever berating it. 'Howard, sit!' the neighbour commands. 'I won't tell you again.' Except she does. Constantly. Howard always has a look of defeat. Though it could be the way his eyebrows are groomed.

You're halfway through elevating your right cheek and furrowing your brow as your face assumes the 'I'm sorry your dog died' expression when you lose confidence. What if Barry is not a dog?

You can't ask when Helen is due back; if Barry is a human, it looks insensitive.

Tamzin continues. 'Yep, we adopted Ken last month. He's a handful.'

Your brain does a quick calculation. Tamzin looks fifty. Too old to be adopting a child.

'They told me he'd have a mind of his own,' she continues. 'But boy, he's a real tearaway.'

Maybe she's adopted a teenager.

'He urinated on the carpet last night. I had to speak to him firmly.'

Ken could be a drunk teenager unable to navigate his way to the bathroom.

'We found him two hours later, hiding under the house, chewing on an old lamb shank,' says Tamzin.

Okay, unless Ken has some serious issues, he's probably not a teenager.

'I have a cat,' you say pointlessly.

'Do you? I'm allergic to cats,' says Tamzin.

Oh god, now you've started a new thread of conversation.

'Anyway, would you be able to check on Helen?' you say.

'Of course,' she says, stretching her fingers like a safe-cracker. 'I will now check with Hamish when she'll be back.'

She punches some numbers in. 'Hey Hamish, when will Helen be back?' She puts her hand over the phone. 'Right, they don't know when Helen will be back. Could be this week. Could be next, but Karen's handling her work and Karen's on a three-day development program.'

A deep red flush flares across your face. The headache, liberated by the spike in blood pressure, detonates across your head. You lean over, grab the picture of the Labrador and tear it in half.

'Grown-up colouring in is stupid,' you hiss.

Odette's eyes widen.

You slam your hands on the desk and yell, 'I have to get this signed off today or tomorrow at the latest, I'm sorry everybody's away and pregnant and their dogs have died, but I have an idea and I don't play golf or live in the cafe, so I need this signed off.'

Tamzin puts down the receiver, and stares at you. The whole floor has gone quiet.

You're holding your breath. The whole floor is holding its breath. Odette picks up the colouring book, leans across the desk and offers it to you.

You exhale. Take the book from her hand. Lower yourself into the chair. 'Sorry.'

She shrugs, smiles. 'I'm practising non-attachment.'

You open the colouring book at a rabbit, pick up a pencil, and begin colouring in the carrot blue. You understand the appeal of staying in the lines. You look up at the office. Everyone's gone back to their work. The moment's over. Of course it is. The wake you leave behind you is shallow. You barely make a ripple. Even your capacity to create a drama is tepid. You're invisible. An afterthought. Not even The Cat takes you seriously.

You colour in the top of the carrot pink. Maybe you should get a dog. Not a pathetic Beagle, but an enormous Great Dane like Bethany's. Then you can haunt local cafes and have it sit majestically next to you, while you guide small children's hands to pat its massive head.

What are you thinking? The Cat would never allow a canine presence in the house.

You slump in your chair. Your throat is sore from yelling; your headache retreats to a nauseating thump.

Odette is still smiling at you. Maybe she thinks you're unstable and is trying to calm you, like a skittish horse. What are you doing sitting here? You don't need a Great Dane. You need to get a grip on yourself.

You close the book, hand it back to Odette. 'I've started on the carrot,' you say.

She looks at your efforts. Nods approvingly.

You straighten your back with an effort. Right, Kat, get a grip on yourself. If not now, when? If not you, who? It's time to go from doormat to diva. These internet inspirational sayings must have lodged themselves somehow in your consciousness, as your inner voice sounds like Oprah.

Anyway, maybe the internet has a point.

You look at your phone, sitting at your elbow. You pick it up, search the calendar for the next networking session. Tick attending. Quinn O'Reilly wouldn't miss a networking session if his life depended on it and, from now on, neither will you.

You dial a number. 'Hey Quinn, top of the morning to ya,' you say. 'It's Kat Mitchell. Like to have a coffee to talk about partnering on my data mining idea?'

THE THING WITH POWER: WHERE DOES IT COME FROM AND HOW DO YOU GET IT?

So, there's a theory that primates (us and our monkey cousins) have great big brains because we live in great big complex social groups. But our great big brains sometimes struggle to negotiate their way around these social mazes. Kat, in an effort to elevate her career, is trying to navigate her way around her corporate social group but is hitting some difficulties. So, how can she negotiate her way around the business of getting what she wants, and what's currently getting in the way?

A bit of interesting stuff about status

During my acting career, I was very interested in the work of Keith Johnstone, who wrote a book called *Impro*.[8] My favourite chapter was one on status. This chapter described the power dynamic that informs much of the communication between people. When rehearsing for a play or a film, many actors, myself included, would explore the ebb and flow of power that pulses underneath the drama. An actor can drill into the psychology of the character and discern whether the character is (a) aware of what's driving them in response to the ever-present power dynamic in the scene, or (b) unaware, in which case they're being driven subconsciously.

Later in my life, when I went into communication consulting, I worked out that the status principles that Johnstone had described in his book were as useful in real life as they were in the theatre.

---

8   Johnstone, Keith (2012), *Impro: Improvisation and the Theatre*, Routledge.

So, back to Kat's drama.

There was clearly a power play between Kat and Tanya, the executive assistant, in that Kat's efforts to meet with the CEO were stymied by Tanya in full gatekeeper mode. If an actor were playing the character of Kat in this scene, she would determine that Kat knew she wasn't winning the battle of wills but was unclear exactly why. This is a common experience. Sometimes we're consciously aware of the power dynamic present in an interaction with another person, and sometimes we're not.

However, the tribal part of our brain is aware of and reacting to barely detectable social signals constantly – signals that our conscious brain is not picking up. Signals about power.

Our brains are picking up signals to do with power all the time.

Whether we like it or not, power is part of being human, and human beings operate on a very subtle level in relation to power. On a subconscious level, we notice who has the power, who's fighting for it and who's happy to relinquish it.

Think in terms of high and low status

In certain contexts, we hold power and in other contexts we don't. Sometimes we need to be operating out of a 'high status' place. Sometimes we need to be operating out of a 'low status' place.

What is high status?

High status involves being assertive and firm, and having control or authority. It can also involve being condescending, aggressive, domineering and superior. Being high status is neither a good nor a bad thing. As with everything, it depends what's driving the behaviour.

Being high status simply means you desire to control your current situation.

In the interaction between Kat and Tanya, Tanya was operating from a place of high status.

What is low status?

Low status involves joy, approachability, empathy, flexibility and friendliness. It can also involve being timid, submissive, apprehensive and overly compliant. Low status in and of itself is neither a negative nor a positive thing; it simply means you respond to the situation rather than being in control of it.

In the interaction between Kat and Tanya, Kat was operating from a place of low status.

Why is it relevant?

It's relevant because our subconscious responses to power drive a lot of our behaviour.

As an actor, being aware of this dynamic meant it would form part of my investigation into the background of a character. I would interrogate the script to try to determine what events in the character's life would have influenced the status with which they met the world. Characters in plays or films are like us – a combination of personality, background and current circumstances.

Most actors know that a character's status bias will affect their physicality – the way they walk and talk, their physical mannerisms and attributes – as well as influencing the other characters on conscious and subconscious levels. The script itself also informs the actor of the sort of language the character uses. Some characters can be described as being low status; others are high status.

This doesn't mean the character has to stay in low- or high-status mode all the time: it just means it's the character bias.

Characters will often surprise the audience by going against type and behaving differently. Think in terms of the mouse that roared, the submissive person finding their mettle or the king who falls on hard times and has to ask a peasant for food. This, again, is like us as everyday humans. How often have you done something totally surprising to yourself? You might even say, 'I cannot believe I did that. That's so out of character.' This is because the circumstances you were in affected you so strongly that you were pushed out of your normal status bias. An example of this is Kat yelling in the office at the end of the chapter. She became so frustrated it pushed her out of her usual low-status bias. However, her reaction wasn't particularly effective.

If we can be in control of our status position, we're more likely to achieve the outcome we're after.

So, back to my process as an actor. Between the script itself and my interpretation of it, I would come up with a character, which was full, rich and hopefully believable – a character reacting to the world round her, a character responding to the swirl of power dynamics in the world she inhabited. This again mirrors us in everyday life. We develop a way of moving, speaking and interacting in the world which is a combination of our personality, history and current circumstances. Some of our characteristics and habits might work well for us while others may not.

So, it's good to examine these physical and verbal habits and see what messages we're tacitly giving to the people with whom we live, work and interact on a daily basis.

People will have confidence in you, or they won't; but if you asked them why they'd probably be unable to explain.

Our feelings are important; however, they should not be allowed free rein to drive our behaviour.

However, there is an explanation. In an evolutionary sense, the limbic system in the brain, which reacts to the power dynamic in groups (back in Miriam's day, when they were roaming the savannah), is alive and well today. As soon as it detects a threat, we're triggered into a reaction. Sometimes we're triggered into a high-status reaction, and other times a low-status reaction. Two different people in the same set of circumstances could have different status reactions.

In the face of an aggressive person, one individual could be triggered into a high-status reaction and become aggressive or authoritarian in return; while another person could be triggered into a low-status reaction and become reticent, withdrawn or apologetic. Kat had a low-status reaction in the face of Tanya's high-status response to her request to see the CEO. 'No threat here,' says Tanya's brain, which is experiencing itself as high status in response to Kat's uncertain and apologetic behaviour.

Context changes everything

So, in the interaction between Kat and Tanya, Tanya was high status because, as the gatekeeper for the CEO, she wields a lot of power over who has access to him and who doesn't. In Tanya's interaction with the CEO, however, she was highly responsive and apologetic. This is because the power dynamic shifted: the CEO was high status, and Tanya was low status.

Much of our relationship with power shifts from context to context.

You might be predominantly high status with your partner, but low status with the butcher; high status with the person who makes your coffee, and low status with one of your direct managers. Sometimes the hierarchy will dictate the status dynamic and sometimes personalities can circumvent positional status. Lisa Miles is below Kat in the pecking order, but Kat feels intimidated by her, so Lisa is high status in the relationship and Kat is low status.

In healthy relationships, the status dynamic moves fluidly from one person to the other and back again.

However, most of us have a bias.

You might have a high-status bias

If you have a high-status bias, being in control might be very important to you. You might find that there are many situations and contexts in which you feel your authority is being threatened, and it's important you assert yourself. If you're having a high-status reaction, regardless of whether it's appropriate or not, it will feel right.

If your limbic system experiences itself as being under threat and you have a high-status bias, your frontal lobe will post-rationalise the emotional response with thoughts along these lines:

- 'Nobody pushes me around.'
- 'I know how to do my job. I don't need to be told.'
- 'We've been doing it like this for twenty-five years.' The proposed changes are stupid.'
- 'I know everyone's been delayed, but I need to get on the next flight. I should be prioritised.'
- 'I won't be taken advantage of.'
- 'Who are you to tell me what to do?'
- 'You've cut into my lane, and I'm going to have to drive you off the road.'

You might have a low-status bias

If you have a low-status bias, being no trouble, keeping the peace and being liked may be very important to you. You might find that there are many situations and contexts in which you feel you have to make way for other people. You're constantly prioritising other people's needs before your own. You may feel easily intimidated and unable to hold a boundary. If you're having a low-status reaction, regardless of whether it's appropriate or not, it will feel right.

If your limbic system has experienced itself as being under threat and you have a low-status bias, your frontal lobe will post-rationalise the emotional response with thoughts along these lines:

- 'I'm not going to get involved in this drama: there's no point.'
- 'I don't want to be any trouble.'
- 'Nobody listens to me anyway.'
- 'If I say that, I won't be liked.'
- 'It's my fault; I probably made him angry in the first place.'

Remember fight-flight-freeze

If you don't recognise that you're in the grip of a limbic system response, you're likely to allow your status preference to drive your response. Unless you unyoke yourself from this emotional response, critical thinking is impossible.

The first step is to recognise it's happening.

In the interaction with Tanya, Kat's brain reacted to stimuli and interpreted that she was in danger. The amygdala, the part of the limbic system that responds to fear, picked up a signal and released the same cascade of chemicals as in chapter 5, when she was having to jump into the skipping rope and speak at the meeting. This time, as she faced off an unfriendly executive assistant, the fight-flight-freeze response meant her brain couldn't tell the difference between a lion coming at her and the unfriendly look on Tanya's face.

Depending on how threatened Kat felt during the interaction, she may have experienced the full set of physiological responses she's experienced before: racing heart, sweaty palms, sweaty scalp (actually, sweaty everything), plus butterflies in the stomach and dry mouth – both signs that her brain is shutting down her digestive system to prepare her for fight, flight or freeze. Or she may only have experienced a couple of these responses, such as her heart beating faster or losing clarity of thought.

Whether it's the whole box and dice or just a hint of the limbic system response, she needs to be aware of it.

Being aware of it is the precursor to managing it.

Again, if you're wondering how to manage the fight-flight-freeze response, revisit chapter 5 and the Tame the Dragon approach. It's not foolproof but it's a really good start to regaining control.

Responding is different to reacting

Reacting is when you allow your limbic system to dictate the status position you will hold in response to a stimulus.

Responding is the positive use of high and low status to get the outcome you want.

People who can utilise high and low status and move fluidly between the two as the circumstance requires are excellent communicators.

How Kat could have better managed Tanya

How could Kat, who has a low-status bias, have held her ground and achieved a better outcome with Tanya? First, she could have recognised that Tanya's response had thrown her, and applied

Tame the Dragon. Next, she could have taken on the persona of her furry friend. Cats are high status, so mimicking their traits will give you the appearance of high status.

Cats are high status. Consider the demeanour of a cat.

If you're wanting to appear to be high status, you could:

- Be as still as possible. Like cats, people with a high-status bias do not expend energy moving around. They are contained physically. Don't jiggle around like a Labrador at a barbeque.
- Be direct and spare with language. State the question, answer or statement directly and use fewer words. Don't endlessly reframe the question and babble on like a five-year-old at a birthday party.
- Embrace the pause. Once you've communicated your question, answer or statement, zip up and sit in that silence – no matter how much you want to fill the void with chat.
- Use direct eye gaze. Think of the way a cat looks at you. Don't stare like you're auditioning for a zombie film, though note that flickering eye movements are also a sign of submission.
- Take up more space. A cat will lounge wherever it wants. It is uninterested in whether you wanted to access the keyboard. People with a high-status bias are more likely to be expansive with their physicality.
- Think of a cat. Still. Direct. Imperious.

If Kat had channelled 'cat', the emotional part of Tanya's brain might have reacted differently. She might have taken Kat more seriously, and not automatically assumed that the person on the opposite side of her desk was lower on the pecking order. Kat could have remained polite and pleasant, but still looked like she meant business.

Now, if you've worked out you have a high-status bias, you may have recognised that elements of it can contribute to conflict in your life. The first thing to do is recognise you've been triggered into a high-status response and apply Tame the Dragon.

Labradors are low status. Consider the demeanour of a Labrador.

You could:

- Think of a Labrador. Approachable, friendly, a lot of tail-wagging, nonthreatening, joyful. Labradors are not pictures of stillness and restraint, and neither should you be. Low status is physically more flexible than high status. Move more.

- Ask questions. Show curiosity about the other person. Allow someone else to dominate the conversation. If you find yourself re-inserting yourself into the conversation and talking about something you're an expert in, stamp on your own foot and go back to being curious about the other person.

- Avoid long, sustained pauses between your statements.

- Take up less space physically. Avoid physical positions like leaning back with your hands linked behind your head, or splaying your legs with your hands on your hips.

- Be more responsive and flexible to other people's ideas. For example, agree to go to a restaurant someone else recommended.

- Listen to explanations offered before giving your reply. Listen to understand, instead of listening to reply.

- Go back to the idea of Labradors. Labradors are the epitome of using low status to get what they want. They are not aggressive or intimidating; rather, the message is, 'I'm adorable but relentless.'

- Avoid being too direct with your eyes. Imagine a Labrador at the dog park being confronted by a Staffordshire Bull Terrier. He would roll on his back and avoid direct eye gaze. If you are trying this, go for the averted eye gaze, but avoid rolling on to your back. It could send the wrong message in a team meeting.

A final word on status

It's easy to get caught up in the negative elements of high and low status. Yes, the downside of high status means a person can be arrogant and domineering, but they can also be compassionate, decisive and inspiring. Yes, the downside of low status means a person can be submissive, timid and indecisive, but they can also be flexible, empathetic and joyful.

The aim is to have control over the status position you take, rather than letting your limbic system choose for you.

The consistency bias

Humans are susceptible to consistency bias. Once we've agreed to something, we're less likely to renege on it. It's why salespeople try to get you to agree that you like whatever you're looking at: you're more likely to buy it. If Kat had managed to get Tanya to agree to securing her an appointment with the CEO, even in the future, Tanya would have felt more compelled to keep the agreement.

The same situation arose with Craig from Legal. If Kat hadn't lost ground and become so defensive about Quinn the Irish Gecko, she could have been more direct in her request.

As usual, some confirmation bias

Of course, it's debatable whether Kat's perception of Quinn's character is accurate. She's in the grip of confirmation bias, cherry-picking available data to confirm what she already thinks of him. By the time she's arrived onto the Risk floor and encountered Odette, she has gone so far down the rabbit hole of confirmation bias – interpreting everything as being against her – she has little chance of regaining ground.

Networking events, argh!

Networking events. Relatively few people actually like them. The reason is that networking events have all the elements likely to set off our fear responses and make us highly reactive to the power dynamics thrumming underneath polite conversations. Your tribal brain is on high alert as to whether you fit in or not. That's what is behind the gut-churning experience when you're standing at a networking event which you've been compelled to attend, and you have to break into that already-established small conversation group.

Not only do you have to talk to people you don't know, but – horror of horrors – you have to sell yourself and your team or organisation. Under such circumstances, your limbic system is under the strong impression that you're not safe; that you won't know what to say; that you'll be rejected. And rejection, to the primitive part of your brain, is not just uncomfortable, but dangerous – hence the disproportionate fear of joining an already established tribe (even if that tribe has only been established for five minutes). To your brain, a group of people already has an exclusive feel to it, no matter how long it has been formed.

So, next time you're at a networking event and you recognise you've been triggered into a limbic-system response, apply Tame the Dragon, then walk on over to that group. Don't put the pressure on yourself to be witty and erudite. It's perfectly reasonable to move into the group and say, 'Mind if I join you?' Then just listen. If you're not in a panic about trying to impress people, you're more likely to make a genuine contribution to the discussion.

Argument from authority

So, what started this whole cascade of events in Kat's life? The CEO's speech. The CEO was in charismatic high-status mode, which automatically fires off the human brain's tendency to fall for argument from authority.

We evolved to form groups and follow the person standing in front of the campfire weaving a compelling story. Argument from authority is so powerful that, in the face of a charismatic individual, many people will literally suspend their critical thinking.

Charismatic people combine high and low status and have a natural ability to tell stories. We are configured to listen to stories. In *Sapiens*, Yuval Noah Harari makes a strong case that it is our capacity to fall in behind a narrative that has distinguished us and allowed us dominion over our planet.[9] Narratives spruiked by politicians prove that, regardless of the veracity of their claims, a large proportion of humans have a strong tendency to believe

9   Harari, Yuval Noah (2015), *Sapiens: A Brief History of Humankind*, Harper.

them. People are constantly amazed at how easy it is to convince others of things that are patently untrue.

We shouldn't be surprised. Belief comes first. Reason comes second.

Primary attribution error

The CEO is guilty of primary attribution error. This is the tendency to attribute personality flaws or character failings to other people's behaviours or mistakes, rather than entertaining the possibility that the situation or environment may be influencing them.

At the same time, in our minds, *our* behaviour or mistakes are not due to any personality flaw or character failing – rather, they're a result of the situation we are in or other external influences.

In the CEO's mind, Tanya was at fault because she's disorganised and incapable of exercising discretionary energy – a fundamental character flaw. His mistake, however – that he told Tanya that he wanted to read the document before it was sent, then didn't tell her he'd changed his mind – was due to the prevailing circumstances, in that he was busy.

This bias arises because we intimately know our own circumstances and how they are affecting our capacity to operate, whereas we are blind to other people's circumstances.

If you start to look for this error in your thinking, you'll find it operating in all contexts in your life. We are much more forgiving of ourselves than of other people.

Be careful of the narrative

Be careful of the narrative you tell as a business. That narrative needs to be supported by reality. Someone like Kat probably has a blind spot around charming, charismatic men. She reflexively trusts the CEO, is optimistically caught up in his vision, and is then disillusioned by the realities of the system. She discovers that the labyrinthine machinations of the bureaucracy involved do not support the idealistic notion of an organic approach to innovation.

Uncompliant Dan's attitude is emblematic of the cultural backlash that occurs when employees become weary of ideas disconnected from the reality of business practice.

Speaking of disconnected ideas, what exactly does 'wellness' mean?

There's been an enthusiastic adoption of wellness and stress-reduction programs by many big companies, but does the research live up to the hype? It's too early to say, but it's important that stress-reduction initiatives aren't rolled out in the hope they'll ameliorate unrealistic demands being placed on employees. If a business is going to implement 'wellness' initiatives, then ensuring the research is solid before they do so is a really good start.

And remember that just because something is Eastern or traditional or natural doesn't mean it's good. As we saw in chapter 4, when Kat was caught up in clean-eating ideas, the positive connotations of words like 'wellness' make it easy for businesses to adopt them without applying the requisite scrutiny. Words like 'wellness' and 'natural' fall into the sphere of the halo effect, and should be treated with scepticism.

Getting smarter

Power dynamics are playing out all the time. If we want to use critical thinking to get the best possible outcome from each encounter we have, we need to manage our emotional reactions first. We are very prone to going with and trusting our instinctive response: whatever we feel feels right. In the highly dynamic world of power, however, questioning and having choice over our status position can mean getting the job, asking for the raise, making the request, holding our own in a meeting or sending back the cold meal (or the cold partner). We're very habituated to our status preferences, but that doesn't mean it's impossible to get a handle on what sends us careening into a status reaction. Learning the signs means we'll have a lot less drama and a lot more success. Basically, we'll spend a lot less time mentally slapping ourselves because things went badly and we know it had something to do with us – we just can't for the life of ourselves work out what!

Get your thoughts straight

Labrador or Cat

We all have a status bias. Now that you've read this chapter, you should have some idea of which contexts send you into either Labrador or cat mode. Work out what your tendency is and be vigilant when you sense it taking over your response when you're under stress.

If you notice you've been sent to either status position, use the Tame the Dragon technique, then use the physical and verbal approaches listed in this chapter.

Pick your Battles

That said, if it's not a big deal, maybe don't get involved in a status battle.

Do You Really Want that Dress?

Be aware of salespeople getting you to agree that you like the dress, the phone, the shoes or whatever it is that you're contemplating buying. Consistency bias means you'll probably feel compelled to buy it once you've agreed you like it.

Aesop's Advantage

Stories are incredibly powerful. If you happen to be giving a presentation, throw in a story. They're way more influential than plain facts.

9

Kat goes away for the weekend

You have been invited on a weekend away. Your best friend Amy suggested it would be good for you to have a break. 'Stop moping around after that pathetic skinny hipster,' she'd said.

She has another new boyfriend. She collects them like stamps. This one's from her work. His name is Manveer. Manveer is inviting some of his friends. You haven't met him, but according to Amy, he's really cool. You should come.

Your imagination endows Manveer's friends with good looks, Jeeps and fair isle jumpers. You'll be drinking red wine in front of a roaring open fire and kicking around autumn leaves. You can post it on Instagram. Your mother will see it. You could be engaged to one of the friends by Christmas.

After berating yourself for engaging in such a traditional, non-feminist view of yourself, you agree to attend the weekend away.

Now Amy is outside, honking. You look out the window and wave. She is double-parked in her 1997 Camry.

You pick up your bag, admire your hair in the hall mirror, throw a kiss to The Cat, call up to Mrs Hume that you're leaving, and run down the stairs and out to the car. You're still carrying that extra 2.75 kilos, but yours is a busy, active life filled with friends and weekends away. Who needs The Hipster?

You arrive at the house. It is dusk and it is picture-book pretty, surrounded by flame-red maples and dogwoods. You are enchanted.

You enter the house and Manveer, the new boyfriend, is standing in the entrance to the lounge room looking at his phone. He is very tall, and exceedingly skinny.

'This is Kat,' says Amy. She stands on her toes, kisses him on the cheek, and heads up the stairs.

You're left standing there. 'Hi, Manveer,' you say.

'Hi, Kat,' says Manveer. 'Welcome to the ranch.' He's looking at you so directly it unnerves you.

'How was your drive down?' you ask. Amy had driven her Camry like a Maserati.

'Very nice, very nice. It's good they've had some rain.' Manveer strikes you as an IT consultant.

'Yes, it's been very dry,' you say. 'Anyway, I'll just go and find myself a bed.'

'All the good ones are gone, unfortunately,' he says.

You avoid contact with IT as much as possible at work. You're now stuck with one of their contingent for the weekend.

'Are you a runner?' says Manveer.

'I'm sorry?'

'A runner. Are you a runner?'

'Um, no.'

'If you want to run tomorrow, I'm doing a 20k at 5 a.m. I'm in prep for the half marathon.'

'Right. No, I'm not a runner.'

'Well, if you change your mind,' he says, 'I have an extra headlamp.'

'Right,' you say. 'Well, I'll just nip upstairs.'

You walk upstairs and down the small hall, past Amy perched on the edge of a large, comfortable, queen-size bed.

You arrive at the last remaining bedroom. It's the size of a closet with a monk-like bed. There is a cross on the wall. You sit on the bed and resist the urge to kneel and pray. You turn on the bedside lamp, look around you, pull your book out of your bag and hold the cover to your cheek.

The first tendrils of worry – that coming was a mistake – curl up from your chest. You feel homesick. You miss The Hipster. You miss The Cat. You're missing Mrs Hume's weekly neighbour dinner. They'll soon be sitting down to Croatian chicken soup, while Mr Kovacic launches into number seven of his Morse code tutorials. Last week, during tutorial number six, you'd all had to practise tapping out what to say if an enemy were approaching.

Nika tapped out, 'Evacuate, evacuate, women and children first.'

Mr Kovacic shook his head. 'Why you evacuate? You on *Titanic*, Nika?'

Nika had rolled her eyes.

You'd successfully tapped out, 'The enemy is near. Lie still and keep your eyes shut.'

'Why keep eyes shut?' Mr Kovacic had demanded.

'Because when you're under the bed, you don't want to see their boots walking past the door,' you'd said. 'It would make you panic.'

'Why they boots walking past door?' asked Mr Kovacic. 'They in plane.'

You'd realised at this point you may have had differing interpretations of what the enemy approaching actually meant.

Mrs Hume had tapped out, 'Bring bandages and waiter', instead of water.

'Why you want waiter?' asked Mr Kovacic, his eyes narrowing. He pounced on mistakes like a jaguar on its prey. 'You in restaurant eating soup when enemy approach?'

Mrs Hume had been unfazed. 'Yes, I meant waiter,' she said, neatly slicing into the Bakewell tart and handing him a plate. 'There has already been shelling and the waiter had shrapnel in his leg and I was going to bandage it.'

Mr Kovacic had reached over to take his plate. There was a moment where they both held one side of the plate each. A look passed between them, then Mr Kovacic broke into a wide smile. 'You should have been spy,' he said. 'You good liar.'

'Lucy Hume,' said Mrs Hume, 'Agent 006.'

You had loved them all so intensely at that point, you had rashly invited them all to Christmas in your flat. You have a photo of their delighted response, including Mr Kovacic waving one of 'big pussy's' paws.

You are sitting on your bed, running your finger over the group photo on your phone, when Amy enters fresh from her large, cavernous bedroom. She looks around and sits on your tiny monk bed, snapping you out of your daydream. What is wrong with you? You're away on a trip. Why are you sitting here stroking a picture of The Cat and your mostly elderly neighbours? Also, your mother will not be happy when you tell her you aren't coming home for Christmas.

'This is cosy,' she says. 'So, let's get the food out of the car.'

You open your mouth to reply, and at this moment the room is plunged into darkness.

You try the switch on your bedside lamp a couple of times. Nothing.

You move to the wall, find the wall switch. Nothing.

Manveer calls from downstairs. 'Amy, the lights are out.'

'Yeah Manveer, I know,' she calls back.

'Where's the fuse box?' he calls.

'I don't know, I just arrived.'

'Where's the instruction manual to the house?'

Amy sighs. 'I don't know, Manveer, I've just arrived. You got here before me.'

The last rays of crepuscular light have deserted the room. You can dimly see Amy rise from the bed and move to the door.

'Well, I can't fix it if I don't know where it is,' he calls up.

Another male voice floats up from downstairs. 'Why you all in the dark?'

'We don't want to be, man,' says Manveer. 'We've blown a fuse.'

'Where's the fuse box?' says the voice.

You wonder if praying will help.

'We don't know,' you call. Your testy tone is new and interesting to your ears.

'Who's that?' asks the voice from downstairs.

'It's Kat. Who's that?'

'Kat Kendall?'

'Kat Mitchell.'

'Oh.' He sounds disappointed. 'Hi Kat. I'm Kyle.' He's probably another IT consultant.

Your longing to be safe back at the neighbour dinner kicks you in the chest.

'Let's go and sort them out,' says Amy.

You tut complicity and follow Amy down the hallway.

The darkness is country darkness. Dense.

You make your way downstairs by the light of your phones. Manveer and Kyle are creeping around the lounge room like thieves in a darkened museum, the beams from their phones in front of them.

You stand in the doorway for a minute or so.

'Well,' says Amy, her voice primly bright. 'If we can't find the house manual we should probably just go outside and look for the fuse box.'

'I'll just ring the owner,' says Manveer. 'Get someone to come.' He dials.

They all stand looking at him.

'No answer,' he says.

There is a pause.

'Oh well then,' says Amy. 'Kat and I will go and look for the fuse box.' It's so obviously a threat, you wait for Manveer to counter her.

'Okay, thanks Amy, I'll try ringing her again. Oh, the headlights are near the front door,' says Manveer.

Amy doesn't move, however. You can see her face, lit by her phone, staring at Manveer.

'Would you like us to collect some wood for the fire while we're at it?' says Amy.

Clearly, she is as unenthusiastic about going outside into the pitch-black spider-infested yard as you are.

Manveer shines the light of his phone towards the fireplace. 'No need, babe, it's a gas fire,' he says. This is your problem with IT people. They're so literal.

'Hey, Kyle, have you seen this?' Manveer has moved on from the fuse box discussion and has positioned his phone close to Kyle's face.

All you can see in the darkened room is faces bathed in its light.

'Oh, he's amazing,' says Kyle. 'Have you seen this? He's Kenyan. They reckon he's the next Kipchoge.'

You glance sideways at Amy. She is still standing in the same position, staring at Kyle. You follow her gaze. She seems to be playing the 'if I stand here staring at you long enough you'll figure out I'm not happy' game. You want to tell her it's futile. You tried the 'stare off into the middle distance looking sad and faintly troubled' game for thirteen months, two weeks and six days and The Hipster still left.

'Come on, Kat,' she says loudly, grabbing you too hard by the forearm. 'Let's go and find the fuse box.'

You try to pull back from her. You are appalled. It's freezing outside, and you loathe spiders. You want to tell Amy to drop the charade and just ask him to go outside. The Hipster blamed you for the missing TV remote for your entire relationship. He never knew it was him who left it places – notably once in the fridge where he'd gone to get a beer – because you never told him. You'd just returned it to the coffee table and hoped he'd work it out. He hadn't.

'Come on, Kat.' She's digging her nails into your arm.

You relent. Shake free from her grip. 'Okay, I'm coming,' you virtually yell.

You're like characters in a pantomime for five-year-olds, giving tips on the plot to their small, underdeveloped brains.

You turn on your phone's torch as Amy ushers you out the front door. You're wearing sandals. The dew has arrived with speedy efficiency, and the wet grass is finding its way into your sandals. Amy is stomping ahead of you, furiously brushing branches aside.

You are now at the side of the house. Something brushes your face. You scream. It's a spider, you know it.

Amy swivels, turns back to you and shines her phone in your face. 'They won't hurt you, Kat, they're harmless,' she says.

'You got a degree in arachnology now, Amy?' you say.

You have always admired people who use sarcasm well. You are not in their ranks.

'Just come on, Kat, it's freezing.'

You look at Amy's retreating back. You adore Amy in a controlled city setting. She's fun in a bar after three vodkas, but as soon as she gets a whiff of the country, she morphs into this disappointed outward-bound team leader. Why did you agree to go away with her?

You are passing the lounge room window. You look in. Kyle and Manveer have now moved to the couch and they're looking at their phones. Their heads look incorporeal, hovering above the glow. At intervals they reach into an invisible bag, then their hands travel to their mouths. Though indistinct, you hear Manveer say, 'Man, seriously, I'm doing the New York.'

You touch the window plaintively with your hand. You are the Little Match Girl; they're the modern-day landed gentry – open fires and roasted meats replaced by the blue light of technology, and chips.

'Why am I going out with him?' says Amy from behind you. You are personally mystified but are hoping this is rhetorical. 'I mean, seriously, what is wrong with me? You know I can't run for the bus.'

It's a good question. What is wrong with her?

'I guess you'll get fit,' you say.

'He's actually really nice,' she says.

'I'm sure he is.'

'Don't be like that,' she says.

'Like what?'

'Not liking him.'

'I like him,' you say.

'He's great when he's not talking about running,' she says.

'Right.'

Amy turns the beam of her phone on you. Shines it in your eyes. 'And the great thing is,' she says, 'he doesn't try to have sex with my friends.'

Heat prickles across your scalp, like a thousand spiders. Your brain serves you up memories of that hot November night, the dance floor, how happy you had been feeling before the incident occurred.

'Amy,' you say, 'he'd had a few beers. He was just mucking about.'

'Kat, he stuck his hand up Louella's dress.'

The trip home in the cab. The Hipster's hot denial.

'Louella's a shocking flirt, we all know that,' you say.

Amy is still shining the phone into your eyes. You feel like you're in a 1940s film noir interrogation scene.

'Kat,' she says, slowly and deliberately, like you're new to English. 'It. Was. Her. Wedding.'

You don't want to think about that night, but your mind is determined to haul you back into the cab on the way home from the wedding. He was furious, pulling at a thread on the cuff of his shirt.

'You're paranoid, Kat. Anyway, I don't even find her attractive,' he'd said.

'Sorry,' you'd said to him. 'Sorry. Sorry.'

You push Amy's phone away from your face, striding towards the back of the house.

You've only gone three steps when you collide with a huge cobweb.

The Hipster didn't speak to you for days after the wedding.

'But you'd go back to him in a heartbeat, wouldn't you, Kat? You'd go back to him tomorrow,' says Amy from behind you.

You flail at the cobweb, which has wrapped itself around you.

'Probably, Amy, I would,' you hiss, frantically brushing your fingers through your hair. 'Then we'd be inside, and he'd be out here fixing the light.'

But Amy isn't listening, she's pointing like a Springer Spaniel. 'There,' says Amy, 'there.'

You follow her finger, and there it is: the fuse box. It's like discovering the opening to Tutankhamun's tomb. You lift the box's heavy steel door upward, flick the switch, and light pours from the house onto the backyard where you stand. All is forgiven between you and Amy. You push The Hipster's behaviour at Louella's wedding back into the dusty far reaches of your brain. Elated by the successful end to your difficult and dangerous quest, you high five. You are Warrior Women. You do not need men to shepherd you through life. You are independent, courageous and autonomous.

When you get back with The Hipster, and he's apologised for previous misdemeanours, you'll be able to tell him about this victory. You run confidently through the well-lit backyard and burst into the house. The two boys are sitting in the same position on the couch, with the addition of a couple of cans of Coke.

'Hey Amy,' says Manveer, not looking up from his phone. 'You found the fuse box.' There is a pause.

'Yes,' says Amy. 'No thanks to you.' Amy's Warrior Woman is leaving the building. Disappointed angry girlfriend is resurfacing.

'Well, I was ringing the owner,' says Manveer.

Another pause, in which Amy stares fixedly at Manveer.

'It was very scary, Manveer,' she says.

'Didn't you take the headlamps?' says Manveer, still looking at Kyle's phone.

Amy exhales theatrically. 'I was freezing, Manveer, and the yard was full of venomous spiders.'

Me too. I went too. Also, a minute ago the spiders were harmless.

'Well, you offered,' says Manveer. Perhaps he thinks Amy will say, 'Oh yes! I did, too. Well, that's alright then.'

She doesn't.

Manveer is now trying to focus on Amy, but his eyes keep straying towards the phone held by Kyle.

'When somebody says "I'll go", they generally mean "Could you please go",' says Amy.

'I think that's right,' ventures Kyle. 'My last girlfriend left me because she said I had zero sensitivity and took everything literally. I didn't think that was true. I don't have zero sensitivity.'

'Man, she wasn't your last girlfriend, she was your *only* girlfriend,' says Manveer. Kyle clips him over the head.

You now want nothing more than to lie on your monk bed, eating chips and reading your book.

Manveer's phone rings. 'Hi,' he says. 'No, it's all good.' He gives the group an optimistic thumbs up. 'We found the fuse box. Right. Yes. Probably the rain. Thanks again.' He hangs up, smiles at Amy.

'We found the fuse box,' says Amy. 'Who's "we"?'

His smile fades. 'Well, I just meant the generic "we"', says Manveer. 'For the purposes of the conversation, she didn't need details on precisely who, just that it had been resolved.'

Amy gives you a 'can you believe I'm having this conversation' look.

'Anyway,' says Manveer, trying gamely to bring the conversation to an optimistic end, 'it's back on so that's good.'

'It didn't come back on by magic,' says Amy, a precursive wobble appearing in her voice.

Oh god, why did you agree to go away with Amy and her IT department? You berate yourself for not demanding clarity on who was coming.

'Just a few of Manveer's friends from work,' Amy had said breezily, invoking a vision of a convertible full of carefree thirtysomethings on their way to long, boozy lunches in wineries.

You're pretty sure the IT guys don't drink, do ride motorised skateboards, and do spend every other waking minute either running or talking about it. You are deeply dispirited.

Amy is now standing, arms crossed, staring at Manveer across the room. Manveer's eyes are still flickering back and forth like a nervous Border Collie between her and Kyle's phone.

She looks angry. He looks mystified.

You recognise your own behaviour in Amy with blinding clarity. The oblique statements. The desperate desire that you will get what you want without having to go through the indignity of asking. The disbelief that your emotional state is not being transmitted and received on some magical wavelength of understanding.

'So,' you venture, 'I guess we'll think about dinner.'

'No, we won't,' says Amy.

Zero-Sensitivity Kyle realises there is mounting tension in the room, and wrests his attention away from his phone. 'We could go into town,' he says, 'save you cooking.'

'Save *us* cooking? Why are *we* cooking?' says Amy tightly.

Kyle moves and stands behind Manveer.

'Kyle, that's sexist. Why should the girls cook?' says Manveer. 'Kyle and I will cook dinner. We'll barbeque the meat we bought.'

'I'm vegetarian, Manveer', says Amy.

'I thought maybe you'd take a break, have a sausage,' says Manveer. Come on, Manveer, you think, you're careering towards the precipice. Veer right, veer left, just for god's sake veer!

Amy walks towards the door. 'After we've risked our lives in the venomous spider–infested backyard, you're now going to make me eat a sausage,' she says.

At least you're included in the narrative this time, but you note the growth of the spider's role. If Amy repeats the story again, you will have done hand-to-leg combat with arachnids the size of dogs.

'No,' says Manveer. 'I just didn't know if you were a full- or part-time vegetarian.'

Amy opens the door. 'Kat and I might just go then.'

Your scalp begins to sweat.

'Go where?' says Manveer.

'Home,' says Amy, with dangerous finality.

Oh lord, you think. It's a four-hour drive. You just got here. It's dark. Amy will probably want to cry, which means her eyes will swell and you'll have to drive.

Amy, on cue, starts to cry.

This seems to alert Manveer that the situation has become tricky. He's across the room like he's in the last ten metres of the Sydney Marathon.

'Babe,' he says, wrapping Amy in his long, gangly arms. 'Sorry, babe.'

Amy is now gushing tears like a geyser. 'It's not that I minded going to the fuse box, it's just that you should have at least offered to go, so I could have said, "No, I'll go". I mean, I'm a feminist and everything, but you took me for granted and you should have checked and thanked me,' Amy babbles.

'Sorry, babe. I'm an idiot.'

In the thirteen months, two weeks and six days you were together, you can never remember The Hipster apologising. Not once. After the recently verified 'inappropriate touching of the bride' incident, you had stood in the doorway of your bedroom holding The Cat. 'I saw you,' you'd said. 'And so did the groom. They'd only been married an hour. You're lucky he didn't hit you.'

'That groom was a pudgy, unfit baby, so good luck with hitting me,' he'd said.

You shook your head.

'The point is, nothing happened, and you need help,' he'd then told her.

You'd begun to sob, out of sheer, blinding frustration.

'I'm sorry, Katty, I refuse to be manipulated by meaningless shows of emotion,' he'd said, taking the car keys off the hall table and heading out the door.

'Those are my keys,' you'd said, wiping your nose on the back of your hand.

He'd closed the door behind him.

So, Manveer may be slow off the mark and not awash with charm, but at least he apologises.

Between Manveer and Amy, the apologising and repeating of the offence goes on interminably until eventually she relents, allows him to wipe mascara from under her eyes, takes her by the hand and leads her upstairs, presumably to the cavernous queen-size bedroom.

You're now standing there, in the doorway, with Kyle.

'I think he means a flexitarian,' he says.

'I'm sorry?' you say.

'Manveer said he thought Amy was a part-time vegetarian. A part-time vegetarian is a flexitarian.'

The four-hour drive home is looking preferable to standing here talking to Kyle.

A noise on the verandah. The door opens behind you. A male is backing in, dragging his suitcase. You see his jeaned legs and feet first. The bottoms of his jeans are tucked into his socks.

'Hey, Michael,' says Kyle. 'Where you been, man? You missed all the action. There was a blackout.'

Michael finishes backing into the room and shuts the door behind him. He remains bent over, taking his scarf off and folding it neatly into his bag. 'Cold out there,' he says.

The last time he saw you, you were climbing over a balcony. You wonder if he'll remember.

He stands up, sees you. 'Hey, Balcony Girl,' he says. He remembers.

You're unsure whether to feel humiliated or flattered. You go for flattered. 'Hi, Sock Boy.'

He looks down at his feet.

'Balcony Girl?' says Kyle.

'Does she use your front door? Last time I saw her she was leaving over a balcony,' says Michael, taking his jacket off.

'No,' says Kyle, backing away like you're radioactive. 'No, she's never used my front door, or balcony door – well, I don't have a balcony, but still – or in fact any door in my house. We've just met.'

You're not interested in him, but you find the rejection from Zero-Sensitivity One-Girlfriend Kyle dispiriting.

You can't be sure, but you think a fleeting look of satisfaction crosses Michael's face.

'Amy and I sorted the blackout,' you say, like a six-year-old doing show and tell. 'We went out in the spider-infested yard in the pitch black and found the fuse box.'

'Wow,' says Michael, touching you lightly on the shoulder. 'That's impressive. It's freezing out there and dark.'

You look up at him. Now *that's* the response you and Amy were after.

He moves past you into the kitchen. You watch him unpack a bag of groceries. He appears to have brought soup.

A strange and long-lost feeling arises in you, a warmth travelling up through your chest and suffusing your face, like a blush without the redness. You put your hand to the shoulder where he touched you and look back into the kitchen where he's unpacking things from his recycled shopping bag. There is a certain quality to him. He's not waiting on a response. His compliment is not part of a bargaining agreement. You don't have to reciprocate.

You look around the lounge room. The gas fire is on. The room looks inviting.

'We're running at five,' Kyle says to Michael. 'Manveer brought the headlamps.'

'Okay,' says Michael. 'You coming, Balcony Girl?'

You had packed your most flattering pair of leggings in case exercise was part of the fun-packed weekend's agenda; but running was still running, and you couldn't see yourself romping through the freezing predawn with a headlamp strapped to your forehead.

'I'm happy to do the croissant run,' you say.

Michael turns around, smiles. For an IT guy, his teeth are good. He's almost handsome.

You wonder if he's brought a fair isle jumper with him.

Maybe tomorrow you can go out and kick some autumn leaves around.

STOP THINKING EVERYBODY SHOULD THINK LIKE YOU – START REALISING THEY DON'T, AND WORK WITH THAT

There's a saying: 'The single biggest problem in communication is the illusion that it has occurred.' How often do you find yourself in an argument with somebody and you say, 'But you must have known what I meant. How could you not have understood?' and they look completely perplexed, like you were speaking a foreign language?

For the amount of words that spill from our mouths on a daily basis, our level of miscommunication is impressive.

What goes wrong? How can we be in the same conversation but interpret it completely differently?

Let me explain theory of mind (in other words, don't assume other people know what you want)

Kat sees elements of her own behaviour in Amy's attempts to communicate with and influence Manveer. Amy's first mistake was assuming that Manveer would understand that her offer to go outside wasn't genuine. She was adhering to the well-worn social convention of saying one thing while meaning another, and believing that the other person would pick up on the inferred meaning.

The intention of a question like, 'Would you like us to collect some wood for the fire while we're at it?' is perfectly obvious to Amy; but Manveer completely misses her sarcastic undertone, and he takes it literally. And so, the trouble starts.

To even begin to assess what another person may be thinking or feeling requires you to have good theory of mind – the capacity to understand that other people have beliefs and perspectives different from your own. Manveer doesn't *ignore* Amy's hints; rather, he doesn't pick up on them. He may not have a high level of social awareness.

People have different levels of social awareness and social fluidity. Don't assume you know what's going on for people, or that they know what's going on for you.

Being socially aware – having a high emotional quotient (EQ) – means being able to pick up both obvious shows of emotion *and* the smaller, less obvious expressions that cross the face. People with social acuity, like Kat, make no conscious effort to pick up large and small expressions. For her, this extreme sensitivity to other people's emotional states is automatic. As we've learnt, sometimes her assessment of that emotional state is accurate, and sometimes it's not. But regardless of the accuracy of her interpretation, she always notices.

People with a low EQ, like Manveer, might miss emotional states entirely unless they are very obvious (like crying). It is also difficult for Manveer to pick up sarcasm and inferential comments in speech. Taking a circuitous route with him in situations may backfire. Here, Manveer missed all the signals, verbal and facial, that Amy sent out, and he didn't realise that she was distressed until she cried. This doesn't make him uncaring or selfish – he just needs a more direct style.

Amy was so involved in her own thoughts and feelings that she expected Manveer to divine what was going on for her. Expecting someone like Manveer to mind-read isn't just a mistake, it's a recipe for disaster.

Yes people, it's the spotlight effect again

If you're very upset about something, it's natural to assume that the other person will know what's going on for you without your having to expressly say it. It's the spotlight effect at play again. Because we are so central to our own worlds, so acutely aware of our own thoughts and feelings, we assume others are, too. We assume they are noticing and judging us.

People do notice and judge, of course; it's the degree to which they do that's the point.

In chapter 7, when Kat was at the party, and in chapter 7, when she was at the networking event, she mistakenly felt more observed than she actually was. She sees the same phenomenon operating in Amy, who's so exquisitely involved in her own feelings that it seems impossible for her to comprehend that Manveer isn't aware of them, too.

Everybody is self-involved and way too busy thinking their own thoughts and feeling their own feelings to be bothered about you.

So, the two principles of the spotlight effect and theory of mind combine to create some pretty difficult communication issues – especially in intimate relationships.

If someone in the relationship has a reduced level of sensitivity around picking up emotions while the other person is under the misconception that their emotional reality is being clearly broadcast, the potential for drama is massive.

So, back to Kat – her old friend avoidance is in attendance

Okay, so you might be asking, why is Kat such a pushover? Also, why do other people's behaviours seem easy to judge from the outside, yet our own behaviour is difficult to assess?

As Steven Novella says in *Your Deceptive Mind*, 'We are mysteries to ourselves.'[10]

We have to return to the basic principle that we are all irrational – that some of our feelings can lead us astray, and our frontal lobes spend a lot of time justifying decisions made in our limbic systems. Like all people who have trouble standing up for themselves, it's easy to look from the outside and think, 'For the love of Mike, Kat, just stand up for yourself.' As per so many instances in this story, her limbic system has been making decisions for her, and her frontal lobe has been busy coming up with some pretty reasonable-sounding post-rationalisations. But remember: that's all they are. Kat will have a thousand reasons for not asking who exactly is coming to the weekend away, whether there's a better bedroom and why she and Amy are the ones going into the spider-infested yard.

She might think:

- 'Why make a fuss?'
- 'It's easier to go with the flow.'
- 'Just accept the situation; I'm lucky to be invited.'
- 'I don't want to be seen as high-maintenance.'

These perfectly reasonable-sounding thoughts will be justifying an emotional reaction to the situation. Being in an environment with potential drama feels unsafe. It feels better, more familiar,

---

10 Novella, Steven (2012), *Your Deceptive Mind: A Scientific Guide to Critical Thinking Skills*, The Great Courses.

to be compliant and avoid making waves. To Kat, pushing back, taking a stand, setting a boundary and holding her ground would feel unsettling, impolite, not nice, perhaps even dangerous. So, she continually suppresses her own feelings, doesn't clarify who else is coming, internalises her discomfort with her room and resentfully agrees to go outside. Amy, on the other hand, takes advantage of Kat's tendencies and is controlling and impatient.

We post-rationalise decisions that we make subconsciously. We do this all the time.

In chapter 8, we learned how Kat's tendency to operate out of a low-status bias stymies her attempts to have her proposal signed off. In this chapter, Kat automatically drops into low status around Amy and the boys. She might not like the result of it, but staying low status feels right.

At the beginning of her story, on the day The Hipster left, Kat held her ground about not wanting to eat vegan cheese. It's a small thing when you're observing from the outside, but the result was disastrous to her: The Hipster left. So, from her perspective (which isn't particularly rational), holding the line about the vegan cheese caused more trouble than it was worth.

Remember also our issues with memory. Emotionally charged events have a greater impact on our brains. We store them better and we have easier access to them than other memories. The Hipster leaving was undoubtedly an emotionally charged event for Kat.

Confirmation bias, again

Kat, still smarting from The Hipster leaving, is now using confirmation bias to confirm that pushing back, or holding your ground, always goes badly. This is the problem with confirmation bias: it narrows your thinking. Instead of looking at all the dynamics in a relationship – which should have alerted Kat that it was not a healthy place for her to be – she allows her thinking to be hijacked. Whereas if, in fact, she were to use critical thinking, she might actually uncover some instances when holding her ground would be productive.

The positive thing about the encounter between Amy and Manveer is that it alerted Kat to her own indirectness. We can often see behaviour in others that we are blind to in ourselves. While observing Amy trying to get Manveer to go outside without directly asking him, Kat remembers she rarely said anything direct to The Hipster. She realises she was engaged in a 13-month mime show. Her reasons for not being direct with The Hipster are complicated, with one driving factor being that she was fearful of him.

Of course, it suited The Hipster to keep Kat quiet and compliant. He could then encourage her to be direct, and freeze her out when she was. This is classic gaslighting – giving someone mixed messages, then punishing them when they get it wrong, which of course they will.

Kat is beginning to develop some critical-thinking skills. She is starting to understand that if she'd managed to be more direct with The Hipster earlier on, she may not have wasted so much time in a pointless and damaging relationship.

Hello again, heuristics

Kat also uses a mental shortcut in this chapter – a heuristic that puts all guys from IT in the same bucket. Her subconscious had a bit of a look through the filing cabinet, pulled out the file called 'Socially Awkward IT Consultants', blew off the dust and settled back for a nice cup of tea. No further thinking required. Through

TV shows like *The Big Bang Theory* and *The IT Crowd*, we've been exposed to the stereotype of the intellectually bright but socially awkward men of the IT and science worlds.

So, the weekend wasn't going so well. Kat's preconceptions about the way men who work in IT are likely to behave were confirmed as soon as she walked in the door. And though it might seem that the boys behaved true to form, how much did confirmation bias, avoidance and a lack of understanding of other people's communication styles contribute to the drama?

As with all stereotyping, there is often some truth to the cliché and it's good to be aware of different capacities for social awareness, so as to adapt your style of communication.

However, assuming all men in IT or engineering or science are going to be socially awkward is unhelpful.

Getting smarter

People aren't mind-readers. The combination of the spotlight effect and the differing levels of theory of mind people possess means we spend a big chunk of our lives thinking other people know what's going on for us and what we want, when the truth is often that they don't. It's easier to look at the other person and conclude that their behaviour is disappointing than to consider that the conflict has something to do with us.

Of course, other people can often be difficult, obtuse or just outright mean. That doesn't mean we shouldn't also work out what our contribution is to any drama.

Easier said than done.

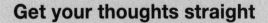

Get your thoughts straight

See What You Believe

Try to be aware of when you're using your own filter to make a decision about who someone is. Watch if your brain is engaged in confirmation bias – this means you will only see the aspects of the person that confirm your stereotype, and discount aspects that don't.

Tell It Like It Is

Watch for times when you assume the other person comprehends what's going on for you or is accurately interpreting what you're saying. This is especially important if you know the person is not good at picking up subtle signals. Drop the subtlety. Be direct.

Partial to Postponement

Are you avoiding something, like a task, a decision or a difficult conversation, then kidding yourself with a realistic-sounding post-rationalisation? Do the thing instead. See if you feel better.

10

The Hipster is back

The Hipster is back. You arrive home to find him sitting on the couch with his back to you, stroking The Cat.

You gasp. He's cut his hair and is wearing a suit. At first, you think he is an intruder.

You begin backing out the door as he turns around and smiles at you, naturally, like he's just returned from a quick trip to the corner shop.

You gasp again. He's shaved his beard.

'You like the clean-shaven look?' he says.

You don't know what to say. Except for the glimpse of him over the bannister at the party, you haven't seen him for eight months.

The treacherous Cat, feigning indifference to The Hipster's patting, moves away from him to the other end of the couch and looks at you.

You refuse to meet The Cat's gaze.

You're still standing at the door.

'What do you want?' you say.

'I bought wine,' he says, waving a medium-priced sauv blanc at you.

'Oh,' you say.

'Your favourite.'

'I don't drink anymore,' you lie.

'Okay,' he says. 'Mind if I do?' The question is clearly rhetorical. He stands and confidently goes to the cupboard where the wine glasses are kept. You wish you'd rearranged the cupboards. 'Nice dress.'

You look down. It's not nice. It's the green floral dress that makes you look fat. You put your hand to your hair, feeling the residue sweat from tonight's gym class. Why did he have to come on a Wednesday? You have Wednesday hair. Why couldn't he surprise you on a Tuesday? Tuesday is your best hair day.

'How did you get in?' you say.

He pulls a key from his pocket and dangles it from his index finger.

You force your legs to move and advance towards him, take the key from his hand, and promptly drop it.

You both lean down at the same time to pick it up, bumping heads.

He picks it up and places it in your palm.

'Anyway, The Cat is happy here,' you say.

'I'm not here about the cat,' says The Hipster, moving towards the wine bottle.

Your heart smacks against your ribs.

The Cat feigns indifference.

A knock at the door, and Mrs Hume's voice. 'Kat, I've a delivery for you.'

A delivery? Maybe he's sent flowers as well. You move towards the door. Open it.

Mrs Hume stands there. Without flowers.

'A delivery?' you say.

Mrs Hume gives you a cryptic look, and peers past your shoulder. 'All okay?' she whispers, with the back of her hand to the side of her mouth. 'I saw him entering the building at 5.45. I made a positive identification even though he was wearing a suit and has shaved his beard. I see why he had a beard. His chin is quite weak. So, he's been in your flat for one hour and forty-five minutes.'

You look back over your shoulder. He is standing at the kitchen bench, drinking the sauv blanc and flicking through your mail.

'He had a key,' you say.

Mrs Hume pulls a deeply disapproving face. 'Well, you know where I am, Kat.' She squeezes your shoulder and looks at you like you've had a recent bereavement.

You become aware of a tapping noise coming from the Kovacics' flat.

'Oh, and I've alerted the Kovacics,' she says. 'They're also on standby.'

The door to Mr Yee's apartment opens minimally. Mr Yee's hand appears and gives you the thumbs up.

'I've also told Mr Yee and his wife.'

'Thanks,' you whisper. 'Tell them I'm fine.' You shut the door and lean on it, wishing you hadn't told the no-drinking lie.

The Hipster has returned to the couch. 'Who was that?' he says, with such casual intimacy you want to swoon.

'What do you want? Rebecca throw you out?' You sound unflinching, brave to your own ears.

'I've bought you something,' he says, walking towards you.

Before his hand has completed the descent into his pocket, your brain has gifted you your life as Mrs Hipster. It has you happily walking out of your recently renovated semi with two children.

A boy of two, Angus, in dungarees, and a girl of five, Matilda, in a ballet skirt. You have apparently just returned from a holiday in the Maldives.

The Hipster hands you an envelope.

You open the envelope while berating yourself for having such a gendered portrayal of your children. You reimagine the scene with the boy wearing the ballet skirt. Your brain is struggling with the cognitive dissonance, however. Angus is not happy. He's holding on to the doorframe, screaming, while you try to cajole him down the path. Parenting is harder than you thought.

You pull two tickets out of the envelope. They're to a Tony Robbins weekend extravaganza, starting tomorrow. You are suspicious. Tony Robbins is a giant. Literally. The Hipster knows that tall people and very large animals leave you cold. Did he really buy them for you?

He's looking at you intently. 'I bought them for you, and then just couldn't ring you.'

You look back at him, feeling an unfamiliar stirring of irritation. 'You understand how a phone works, right?' you say. 'Touch screens have really simplified the process of dialling.'

He is sent off kilter. Your truculence is foreign to you both.

'They were really expensive,' he says plaintively.

'Why don't you take Rebecca?' You jut out your chin and narrow your eyes, like a feisty female detective in an interview-room scene. In the myriad 'Return of The Hipster' scenarios you've concocted, not once did he waltz into the flat using his own key and present you with tickets to a Tony Robbins weekend extravaganza.

He looks sadly at you. 'Rebecca and I... Our life goals aren't aligned.'

You hand him back the envelope and walk to the kitchen bench. You check your Fitbit. You've been home fifteen minutes already, and he hasn't apologised. Tell him to go. Ask him to give you back your washing machine, dryer, coffee table, Moroccan teapot and matching glasses and remote. Show him the door. You're busy. If he wants to see you, he should use the proper channels. Call you. Text you. Ask you to dinner. Tony Robbins tickets?

Jesus. Just tell him to go. Do it. Tell him to go.

But he's wearing the jumper you bought him, and his aftershave keeps wafting towards you.

'So, do you want some dinner?' you say.

'We could go get some,' he says.

'I'm in a new relationship,' you say.

'Oh, with who?'

'Whom,' you correct.

'Whom?'

'Michael. He's from IT. He's really nice.' As the words come out, you consider the possibility that you might mean them.

He moves back to the couch, toying with the remote.

Hang on, the remote? 'Is that the remote?' you say.

'Oh yeah,' he says. He turns to you at the bench. 'What's with the tapping next door?'

You realise the tapping is going on intermittently. You don't answer. You're trying to work out whether to dig into the saga of the remote.

The Cat moves towards him.

He takes a strip of beef jerky from his jacket and shares it with her. He offers you some. 'You eating okay?'

'What happened to the veganism?' you ask.

'Oh yeah, well, Kitten, I was tired all the time. Figured out humans need meat.'

Kitten. He just called you Kitten.

He moves towards you. Touches your cheek. 'You look tired, darling.'

Tired, yes, you're so tired. So very tired. Tired from day after day in the corporate trenches. Tired of rice crackers. Tired of exercising and trying not to get fat. Tired of missing him. You could shut your eyes and lean forward and lay your head on his shoulder.

'So, is President Cat still terrorising the neighbourhood?' he asks.

You both turn and look at The Cat. She is now sitting on the kitchen bench, licking one paw. Considering her options.

'Yes,' you say. 'She rules the complex with an iron paw.'

You both laugh. His eyes crinkle. It's like Rebecca from The Real Estate and the last eight months never happened.

No, Kat. No. Stop it.

You move away from him, resolute about not being a pushover. He betrayed you. He has to say he's sorry.

'What's with the suit?' you say.

'Corporate life coach. Helping others to live their life on purpose.' He pauses. 'I saw Samantha.'

'My sister Samantha?'

He nods.

'Where?'

'Alexandria,' he says.

'Why was she in Alexandria?'

'I don't know, Kat. That's not the point.'

He dislikes his stories being interrupted. He stands and looks at you intently, brushes a hair from your forehead. He smells fantastic. You're back in the centre of his gaze. Nobody has ever looked at you like this. You're the only person in his universe. If you could just hold this moment: stay here forever. This is what you missed. This is why you'll take him back.

You exhale slowly. Relax. Realise you've been holding your breath.

'Kitten, someone as beautiful as you doesn't deserve to be lonely.'

Your chest tightens. Lonely? No. No. No. Lonely people are not appealing. Stupid Samantha has inferred you're lonely while standing in the street in Alexandria. You want to project busy. Occupied. Frantic. Juggling two phone calls at once at the tail end of the day. Jumping in a taxi after leaving work late, to meet your friends in a city bar, before kicking on to the new Japanese restaurant in Surry Hills, before jumping in an Uber to the airport to fly to Port Douglas for the weekend, for a conference and also a wedding.

Not sitting at home with his Cat, fielding concerns from your elderly neighbours.

Younger and Happily Engaged to a Property Lawyer Samantha will pay for this.

He moves away from you, looking at his phone.

The tapping is still going on. They must be putting pictures of their entire extended family on the wall.

'I'm going out to a party soon. I forgot,' you say.

'Anyway, Kitten, I hadn't seen Sam since we broke up. What are the chances?'

'We didn't break up. You slept with Rebecca from The Real Estate then left me.'

'So, I'm mid-session with a client,' he continues, 'talking about his relationship, and it hit me like a bolt of lightning. I thought, I can't be advising others on their life purpose without getting my own house in order.'

Does he mean you are his house?

'I was meant to meet you, Kitten, then lose you, then find you again. I think this is our path.'

'You didn't lose me,' you say. 'You slept with Rebecca from The Real Estate during a mould inspection, then left me for her. Also, you took the couch and the remote, and other things that weren't yours.'

He touches the arm of the new couch. 'Nice.'

Nice? It's mustard with brown piping. It's hideous. You'd stood in the showroom of the furniture shop, holding The Cat, sobbing to the salesman that you didn't care what it looked like, you needed something cheap because your boyfriend had left you and taken the couch, and you and The Cat were sitting on dining chairs to watch TV. The salesman had looked at The Cat for confirmation. The Cat had looked away. 'It's his Cat,' you'd offered as explanation.

The Hipster is reaching into his pocket again. 'Here's what I really wanted to bring you.'

There's another knock at the door.

You reluctantly open it. Mrs Hume is standing there. Behind her, Mr and Mrs Kovacic, Mr Yee and his wife, and Nika bringing up the rear.

'I'm okay,' you hiss. 'Really, I am.'

'You want me to get rid of boy?' whispers Mr Kovacic, looking past Mrs Hume into the room.

'Dad, settle down,' says Nika, giving you a half-apologetic, half-encouraging smile.

You narrow the opening of the door.

Mrs Hume elbows Mr Kovacic in the chest.

'Mr Kovacic, we agreed it's best if I'm spokesperson,' says Mrs Hume.

Mrs Kovacic is beaming at you. 'Yes, Kat, Mrs Hume is the speaker,' she says, laying her hand on Mrs Hume's shoulder reverentially. Mrs Hume, the Patton of the flats, strategising over maps with her loyal generals.

'Okay, but did you hear my tapping?' says Mr Kovacic.

'Tapping?' you say. You look back at The Hipster. He's looking impatient. You roll your eyes in the direction of the neighbours. 'Another bin dispute,' you mouth to him. You look back.

Mr Yee pipes up from the back. 'Tell him The Cat is happy here,' he offers.

'I don't think that's relevant,' says General Hume tersely.

Mr Yee looks crestfallen.

You feel disloyal about the bin comment.

'Kat?' calls The Hipster.

If the second gift is more tickets to see motivational speakers with gigantism, you'll throw him out. However, if it's an engagement ring, you haven't got time to stand here at the door.

You have weight to lose and a wedding to plan.

'Coming,' you say.

You can see General Hume is not happy. Her battle plan is failing. She will temporarily retreat, but there will be a regrouping in the bunker.

'Honestly, I'm fine,' you say, smiling brightly to indicate how fine you are.

'She's fine, guys,' says Nika. 'Let's leave her alone.'

She attempts to pull her mother away from the door, but Mrs Kovacic is immovable. Nothing will distract her from her post. As you shut the door, they are all still standing there in their phalanx. Their concerned camaraderie, though vaguely humiliating, has nevertheless bolstered your confidence.

You turn towards The Hipster, leaning on the back of the door.

'What have you got for me? Tickets to Jordan Peterson?'

He walks towards you, kisses you on the cheek and places in your hand... a box. The aftershave is definitely the one you gave him.

You undo the ribbon. They can all come to the wedding. Mrs Kovacic can make the dress. Nika can be your maid of honour, Mrs Hume can organise security. Mrs Yee can...

It's a necklace.

You untether the necklace from its box and hold it up. It has a pattern of intricate, densely packed chips of crystals. Rose quartz. It's pretty. Sweet. You peer closely at it. Out of the swirl, two letters form: 'R L'.

'This says R L.'

'Yes, it does,' he replies.

'What's it stand for?'

'Real Love,' he says, smiling.

You look at him. His eyes are a deep green-brown. You stare directly into them, trying to divine if he is genuine.

He looks back at you, without guile. Then he smiles, and you are reacquainted with his tiny teeth.

Then you know. You are sure. He's given you Rebecca's necklace. Rebecca Lacombe.

'Did you buy this for Rebecca?'

He looks away sorrowfully, moving across the room to The Cat. He strokes her under her chin. The Cat, already struggling with an image problem, now looks like Mussolini, her chin up. If she had lips, she'd be pouting. They both look at you, united in their disappointment.

'What happened to us, Kitten?'

'You left me for Rebecca from The Real Estate.'

There is a long pause.

'Did you ever ask yourself why?'

You feel faint. He is not here to apologise. He's here to blame you. This is your fault. It's always your fault. Your breath is trapped in your chest like bellows that are stuck halfway. You can't breathe in or out. Your scalp is fielding sharp, cold electric shocks that travel across your head in a disorganised Mexican wave.

The Cat, finally calling her pick, jumps off the counter and wreaths herself around your legs.

'You have terrible trust issues, Kat.'

You recover slightly. 'You cheated on me, and not just with Rebecca from The Real Estate. I have good intelligence that I was right about you at Louella's wedding.' Good intelligence. Why do you sound like you're in the middle of a police drama?

'Amy's behind that gossip, isn't she?' he says. 'She was always trying to break us up. She had a real thing for me.'

'Anyway,' you say, 'the pudgy baby groom has given Louella a baby. They're very happy. And he's lost weight.'

What are you talking about? How did you get to Louella's husband's weight loss?

'Look, I know I was off purpose back then,' he says. 'I was struggling with spiritual nullification, but at least I was living.'

You doubt spiritual nullification is a thing. If it is a thing, it shouldn't be. It sounds awful.

'What were you doing back then, Kat?'

'Pilates?' you offer.

'Kat, who are you? Half of our problem is you don't know who you are.'

Why are you still standing here in your living room with this man who is justifying his appalling behaviour by blaming you? You know it's not going to be any different. Are you so desperate to have him back you'll put up with this?

It looks like it.

'Anyway, Kitten. None of it matters. I love you.' He walks towards you, takes the necklace from your hand, turns you around, lifts your hair, clasps the necklace around your neck and kisses you on the top of the head. He loves you. He will forgive you for not knowing who you are.

Your future as a family of four returns into view.

He puts both hands on your shoulders, turns you around and looks you dead in the eye. 'I love you,' he says.

Threads of happiness weave up through your chest. A laugh escapes you. All will be well. Your life is back on track. You've successfully raised Angus to be a gender nonconformist. He twirls down the path in his tutu. You put your hand to your throat. Touch the necklace.

The Hipster kisses you on the nose. 'Come on, darling, let's get dinner,' he says.

You move towards him. Put your arms around his neck. You see your bookshelf over his shoulder. The book *Your Partner, Your Teacher* winks at you. Why are you prevaricating? There's learning in this. For both of you. He's right. You were part of the problem. You'll go to dinner, acknowledge that and tell him a thing or two about his behaviour.

He'll listen. All will be good.

'What are the Lebs doing? Renovating?' says The Hipster.

You realise the knocks have restarted. You remember you hate the way he talks about the Kovacics. You take your arms from around his neck.

The sounds are now becoming more insistent. Your brain begins to sort the random noise into a pattern. Then it clicks. It's Morse code.

Dah dit dit dah dah dah dah dit.

The Hipster cuts across the tapping. 'Kitten? Do you want to go?' He's making it hard to decode.

'Shhh, I'm listening.' You move towards the wall. Lay your palm against it. The sounds begin to make sense in your brain. Words are forming.

Dit dit dit dit dit dit dit dit dit dah.

DON'T BELIEVE WHAT BOY SAY. HE IS SHIT.

You smile to yourself and begin to tap out your reply.

Dah dit dit dah dah dah.

And as you're tapping it out you turn back and look at him. He's sitting on the hideous replacement couch, flicking through channels with the remote. You are hit with such a blinding realisation that you have to stop tapping and lean on the wall.

It's not you. It's him. You are not fat, and even if you were that would be okay. You are an intelligent, funny, kind person and you're really good at your job. He, on the other hand, is a liar, a philanderer and a thief with tiny teeth. The problem is not you.

You want to ring Rebecca from The Real Estate, and every other girl who's been with him. 'It's not us,' you want to say. 'It's him. We're just interchangeable pawns in his game.'

Well, actually, it could be Rebecca from The Real Estate's fault as well, but it's still probably mainly him.

THANKS, you tap out. HE'S GOING SOON.

The Cat is sitting in between The Hipster and the TV, blocking the screen.

'Hey, Cat, get out of the way,' he says to her.

'Why didn't you give her a name?' you say.

He looks at you. 'Why didn't you?' he says.

'I did,' you say.

'Well?'

You pause. All available cat names have temporarily escaped your brain.

'Come here, Susan.'

'You called the cat Susan?'

'Yes,' you say.

The Cat turns her back on you.

You walk towards The Hipster, take the remote from his hand, go to the front door and open it. Mrs Hume, the Kovacics and the Yees are still standing there. You smile at them.

'We going?' The Hipster says.

You turn back and face him. 'I'm not,' you say, 'but you are.'

He looks at you. You pick up his backpack.

He picks up The Cat. 'I was going to call her Felix,' he says, scratching her under the chin.

You hand him his backpack.

'You really want me to go?' he says. He looks mystified.

He looks past you at your neighbours. The Cat jumps out of his arms.

You take off Rebecca from The Real Estate's necklace and pass it to him.

He weighs the necklace in his hand.

'You're not serious,' he says.

'She's dead serious, mate,' says Mr Kovacic, from behind Mrs Hume.

'Dad', says Nika, 'settle down.' She smiles at you over the shoulder of her mother. 'Kat knows what she's doing.'

The Hipster's face hardens. His nostrils whiten. His top lip stretches over his small teeth. He rubs his hand rapidly over his hair. You notice some thinning on top. He would hate that. He looks at Nika. Your stomach tightens. 'What,' he says to her, 'would you know about relationships? You ever been in one?'

Mrs Kovacic must have been athletic in her day because she's across the room and poking The Hipster in the chest before you can blink. 'Yes,' Mrs Kovacic says, 'she has been in relationship. She in lovely one at the moment.'

The Hipster takes a step back.

'And you know what else, bully boy, her girlfriend doesn't throw things at her or run off with real estate agents.'

'Oh god, Mum,' says Nika.

The Hipster bares his tiny teeth, looking down at Mrs Kovacic.

He turns towards you. 'You need a bunch of Lebs to tell you what to do, Kitty?' he says. 'How about just once in your life you make a decision for yourself?'

Mrs Kovacic hisses through her teeth.

Mrs Hume grips the doorway. Mr Kovacic takes a step forward. Mr Yee puts a warning hand on his arm.

The Hipster leans in; holds your chin. His face softens. 'We would have had the most beautiful children,' he says, kissing you softly on the forehead.

Angus and Matilda float across your vision. They're sitting in the back of a large four-wheel drive, both waving happily at you. How nice of The Hipster to take them out to the park, you think, so you can have some 'Me Time'. Then your gaze shifts to the front of the car. Why is Rebecca from The Real Estate with her bouncy ponytail and perfect skin driving? Whose fantasy is this? Rebecca turns back and smiles at the children. The Hipster sits in the front seat, his hand on Rebecca from The Real Estate's knee. You are not their mother. Besides anything else, their hair colour is wrong. You would think at least one of your children would have dark hair.

You look at The Hipster steadily.

He's smiling softly at you.

'They're Croatian,' you say.

'What?' he says.

'The Kovacics are not from Lebanon,' you say. 'They're Croatian.'

He abruptly swings his backpack onto his back and turns back to The Cat. 'You coming... Susan?'

The Cat jumps onto the couch and commences licking one paw.

He gets to the door, turns backs and looks at you.

You dig your nails into your hand.

He looks sad.

Here's your last chance to chuck Rebecca from The Real Estate out of the four-wheel drive.

'Listen,' you begin.

He interrupts. 'If you don't think you'll be coming to the Tony Robbins weekend, let me know and I'll see if someone else wants the ticket. They're expensive.'

Your resolve hardens, and your heart closes over the last molecule of hope.

Rebecca can have him.

Then, you feel something for him you've never felt before.

Pity.

Because you won't be going to dinner.

You won't ever be Mrs Hipster. And you won't be giving back The Cat.

He walks out the door, past the neighbours.

Mrs Kovacic squeezes your shoulder. 'Don't forget I left strudel in fridge,' she says.

She walks to the door. 'Come on, Lucy,' she says, taking Mrs Hume's arm. 'Time for sherry.'

Mrs Hume smiles at you and closes the door behind her.

The Cat looks at you.

You pick her up and put her on the kitchen counter. 'I'm sorry I said your name was Susan.'

You feel she forgives you. You go to the window and watch The Hipster walking away from your building. He's on his phone. Probably trying to shift the ticket. You see your reflection in the window. For the first time in a long time, you don't turn sideways to see how your stomach looks sucked in.

You *do* know who you are. You're Kat Mitchell. You're thirty-three years old. You don't know what you weigh, and tonight you will cook dinner for your neighbours.

KAT LEARNS HOW TO SAY 'NO'

This is where the rubber hits the road.

Try this quick quiz.

You've made a delightful meal for your boyfriend. As usual, he's two hours late. When he arrives, he says he was held up at work, his phone was on silent and he lost track of time. As he kisses you hello, you note alcohol on his breath, inexpertly covered up with minty breath freshener.

Do you:

a. Smile brightly, pull his dinner out of the oven and pour him a glass of wine?

b. Smile brightly, pull his dinner out of the oven and pour him a glass of wine laced with dog sedative?

c. Smile brightly, pull his dinner out of the oven, throw it at him, pour him a glass of wine and drink it yourself?

d. This quiz doesn't relate to you, because the first time he did it, you calmly sent him home, deleted him from your phone and ate the meal on your own in front of Netflix.

If your answer is a, b or c, read on.

Why do we stay in rubbish relationships?

Whenever we're confronted with someone staying in a disastrous relationship, we shake our heads in amazement and ask how it is possible that the person (often a woman) doesn't see the truth and leave? We all know people who go from crappy relationship to crappy relationship. Who knows, you may be one of them.

Many of us are highly talented at finding ourselves in rubbish relationships, on the receiving end of crappy behaviour by the partner, then taking responsibility for everything that goes wrong.

As we've seen over the course of the book, there are many flaws in our thinking that lead us to the land of poor decision-making. Allowing yourself to get entangled with a narcissist is an example of flawed thinking, leading to terrible consequences.

Narcissists and those who love them

Kat's Hipster displays the classic characteristics of a narcissist. He's charming, good-looking and really attentive at the beginning of the relationship. He just can't keep the attention up for long because, at the end of the day, it's all about him. He's well-practiced at manipulating women to get what he wants. He has an inflated sense of his own importance and desirability, and he can't self-reflect on his own failings.

Kat is a prime target for his sort of seduction. She is anxious and a people pleaser, and desire is a powerful force. She wants to believe him when he says he loves her. She wants the relationship to be the idealised one she has dreamt of, so she goes to great lengths to justify his appalling behaviour.

Read quality literature. Good writers have a better grip on the human condition than most gurus.

Cognitive dissonance

The Hipster's questionable behaviour causes Kat some cognitive dissonance.

Cognitive dissonance is having inconsistent, often contradictory beliefs, values or ideas. Kat becomes uncomfortable when new evidence challenges her idea of who The Hipster is as a person. So, to relieve the discomfort, she rationalises her doubts away.

Here are some of the behaviours that Kat rationalised away (they should be a red flag if you're ever a recipient of them):

- He yelled at her. (There is no justification for someone yelling at you. Ever.)
- He demeaned her.
- He tried to control her weight.
- He was unfaithful.
- He helped himself to her assets.
- He forced responsibility for his cat onto her.
- He let himself into her apartment after not seeing her for eight months.
- He went through her mail.
- He blamed her for his unfaithfulness.
- He gave her gifts he'd bought for someone else, then lied about it.
- He was sexually inappropriate with someone then denied it.
- He gaslit her.

Confirmation bias

There were plenty of signals along the way that Kat was in a relationship with a narcissist, but confirmation bias allowed her to see only what she wanted to see. And what Kat wanted to see – so she could justify staying in the relationship – were examples of her own failures. She wanted to prove to herself that she was to blame for the problems in the relationship.

The Hipster was more than happy to support this version of the relationship. His modus operandi was to constantly imply that any problems in the relationship were caused by Kat and her many flaws.

Beware of being pulled in by charming people who promise a lot.

But Kat was not who she had been eight months prior.

So how did she do it? How did Kat finally say 'no'?

Kat's limbic system and frontal lobe fight to the death

Kat's limbic system and frontal lobe during this last conversation with The Hipster were like two sumo wrestlers hunkered down, arms around each other's shoulders, fighting to get the other one out of the circle. The fight was gargantuan. Kat's limbic system was fully awash with promise of renewed love, while her frontal lobe was trying to navigate its way around all the usual cognitive traps.

But the critical-thinking part of her brain had developed some muscle. The experiences of the past few months had strengthened her critical-thinking skills. She had better insight into herself and the people around her, so when The Hipster returned, she had more difficulty rationalising away his bad behaviour.

Bad behaviour is telling, but kind behaviour is telling, too. Having her neighbours concerned and involved affected Kat at a deep, subconscious level. They provided her with a perspective that challenged the emotional part of her brain. Kindness and concern can punch through the walls your own brain puts up to keep you from the truth. The neighbours genuinely cared about Kat and had formed a well-grounded opinion that The Hipster was not a good and kind person. If you really want to develop your critical-thinking skills, you need to seek out opinions that don't concur with your own – especially if you feel your emotions leading the charge. Kat's neighbours forced her to listen to her doubts, which normally struggled to be heard above the shouting of her desire.

Of course, the signs of The Hipster's true nature were there right from the start, but she'd allowed her thinking to be hijacked by dodgy philosophies like, 'The Universe is trying to teach you something in this relationship.'

As we've discussed over the course of the book, the universe isn't trying to teach you anything. It doesn't care about you. If you're in a relationship that's unhealthy, stop complicating the issue by overlaying it with magical thinking.

Kat saw the truth in the end by being supported emotionally and using her critical-thinking skills, supplanting her emotional brain with her capacity to discern and evaluate.

Belief comes first. Reason comes second.

Men with half-grey stubble who post videos of themselves standing in the forest spouting meaningful-sounding poetry are not qualified to give advice on how to live a good life.

Getting smarter

Everybody wants to be loved. That may be an obvious statement, but the drive is so strong in us that the effort it takes to override our emotional brain is huge.

In literature, TV, films and the lives of our friends, we are surrounded by examples of love gone wrong. However, the analysis of why they go wrong and what we can do about it is not usually very helpful or accurate. Our friends may be well-meaning, but their advice is often not well-founded. The truth is, we often lurch from one unhealthy relationship to the next without any understanding of what is going on.

It doesn't have to be that way. By being on the lookout for flaws in our thinking, we can start to reason with the emotional part of our brain and demand more from the people who are currently sharing our lives.

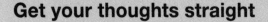

Get your thoughts straight

It's All About Him

Are you discounting or forgiving negative, destructive behaviour in your partner? Being jealous and critical and correcting your behaviour is not an expression of love: it's control. The research tells us that all domestic violence starts with the partner exhibiting coercive or controlling behaviour. The sooner you recognise the red flags, the earlier you can get out of the relationship. It's not going to improve.

The Uncomfortable Truth

Seek out opinions from people who you suspect may have a realistic appreciation of your partner, even if you think you might not want to hear what they have to say.

Neighbourly Love

If your neighbours are reasonable people, reach out to them. There's a lot of evidence that being plugged into a community is one of the most important things you can do for your health.

Conclusion

We all have a view of the world that is highly subjective, cluttered with our own subconscious biases, filters and deeply rooted belief systems.

I hope, as you've read Kat's story, examples from your own life have sprung to mind. All of us, no matter how intelligent we are, fall victim to our cognitive biases. Like the wizard in *The Wizard of Oz*, the subconscious part of our brains is busy pulling levers and pushing buttons, driving our behaviour from behind a thick, opaque curtain. So, go on, pull back your curtain and have a good look at the goings on behind it. I guarantee you'll find it fascinating.

About Annie

The possibility of writing a book was always sitting in the back of Annie's mind; but, being easily distracted, she became waylaid by an acting career. Things were further complicated when she founded a professional development business.

Her acting career saw her performing in major theatre productions across Australia, as well as in most of the Australian TV dramas of the 1990s and early 2000s. She seems to be mainly remembered for running naked in pursuit of a toddler across the stage of the Australian production of *Mum's the Word*. She is still approached by women from Sydney's Northern Beaches who want to reminisce about this event. This is not entirely welcome.

Aside from the naked running, she has spent the last 20 years building COUP – a corporate development and communication consultancy – with her husband, David. They have pioneered groundbreaking, skills-based training drawn from theatre practices, critical thinking and business principles. This has been delivered to hundreds of companies across Australasia in finance, professional services, pharma, resources, telecoms, FMCG, government and utilities, and the profit-for-purpose sector.

In the course of her work, Annie has written, directed and performed in countless corporate dramas, confirming her suspicion that drama abounds in business – much of it sucking the lifeforce out of teams and impeding progress. She believes the difference between good drama and bad drama is critical thinking and effective leadership. She has trained and coached literally thousands of female leaders to develop evidence-based perspectives and the courage to speak up.

Listening to myriad stories her clients have shared, it became blindingly obvious to Annie that the advice offered to women – to resolve issues, be valued for their expertise and experience and enjoy the life and career they wanted – is often misleading, simplistic or just plain wrong.

Annie became deeply irritated and dispirited by the New-Age nonsense, pseudoscientific health offerings and mind-numbing serves of magical thinking she encountered. She found solace in the sensible, humanitarian perspectives of the sceptics, including Sam Harris, Steven Novella, Michael Shermer and Richard Dawkins, and insights into brain function and behavioural economics from Daniel Kahneman and Dan Ariely.

While she found their explanations, corrections and cautions compelling, Annie observed that information about critical thinking wasn't easily accessible. The science can be somewhat impenetrable and, yes, the loudest sceptics seem to be male.

One day, while waiting for the first subject of a corporate role-playing session to arrive, Annie began tapping at her keyboard and the story of Kat began. She was driven by the desire to illuminate the fact that a lack of understanding of our cognitive flaws and unconscious biases can literally ruin our lives.

Annie lives on Sydney's Northern Beaches with her husband (and business partner), her workout buddy and shopping companion daughter and their surprisingly enormous Groodle. Her son visits occasionally to have his clothes washed, consume some vegetables and pat the Groodle.

She can be found at Code 5 gym in Brookvale most days, where she laughs as much as she lifts. She credits this activity with keeping her catastrophic thinking under control (OMG! We're all going to die!), and it gives her tacit permission to drink quite a lot of wine.

She would like it if a lot of women read this book and it made things better for them.

Acknowledgements

This book would have remained filed away on my computer under 'Book' were it not for the unrelenting encouragement of my friends, family, business associates and dogs. The dogs' encouragement was more tacit but counted tremendously. Thanks Hero, Bear and Ryder.

To Anita, for having to endure daily 'Do you think I should write this book?', 'I don't think I will write the book', 'What if people hate the book?', 'Why did you encourage me to write the book?' conversations. Sorry and thanks.

To Katrina Groshinski, Kate Cato, Jenny O'Farrell and Jen Dalitz. Previously filed under business associates, now in my phone under 'friends'. Thanks for the belief.

To Melita, Rowena, Juanita, Lucinda, Merridy, Emma, Kate, Deb, Pete, Lisa and Gail. You ladies have listened, laughed and supported me more than you know. I know about eight Lisas. This is for all of you.

To Zena Shapter, for doing the first edit and telling me to keep at it.

To Cathy Ebert, whose perfect blonde bob I covet. Thank you for your supervision and encouragement, and for ensuring the psychology is accurate.

A big thanks to Dagmar Schmidmaier, for giving me the push I needed.

To the Australian Skeptics, for providing me with my happy place.

To Michelle Wolven and all the ladies of the Chief Executive Women Leaders Program, for confirming that serious stuff is best swallowed with a funny pill.

Thanks to Jaqui Lane, my book adviser, who's like the Year 12 prefect I never got to be: friendly, pragmatic and super helpful, but woe betide you if you drop rubbish in the corridor. I can't thank you enough for pushing me towards my delightful publisher, Lesley Williams, who ascertained there are enough smart women who want to make better decisions to warrant putting these ideas into print. Eternal gratitude to you both.

To Brooke Lyons, my super-lovely, smart editor. Thank you for sending back the edits with reassuring LOLs in the margins, and the pictures of Sooty. He is going to be the star of my next book.

To my Code 5 buddies, for managing to have opinions about book covers and titles while deadlifting 20 kilos. You go girls.

To Georgie, my Ho for life, and Steve, for believing I could write.

To my Allambie book club, for liking my book better than Richard Ford's *The Sportswriter*.

To Katrina, for your vice-presidential scriptwriter's eye, and for being one of the funniest people ever.

To the AHTPBC, for being everything.

To darling Odile, for the days and days spent in your kitchen, throwing words and accents about and screaming with laughter over tea, then wine.

To my brother Paul, for believing in me.

To my daughter Lily, whose scientific expertise and quiet scepticism confirmed my belief that science is where it's at. Thank you for the endless hours answering the most basic tech questions. The fact you never said 'What is WRONG with you?' in the face of me NEVER knowing where I'd saved the last draft is testament to your patience and magnanimity.

To my son Lachie, whose superlative language skills, analytical brain and understanding of structure corralled my meanderings into something like a book. Thanks for the careful editing, encouragement and love.

To my mother, who thought I was marvellous no matter what.

To my father, who believed in nothing without proof.

To David. I live the delightful life I lead and have had the breathing space to tap out this book because your quirky brilliance, intensely kind nature and workaholic tendencies have always kept our whole family ticking over.

Thank you for your wordsmithing.

Thank you for ensuring we didn't have to move into a caravan in Narrabeen.

Thank you for still admiring me and laughing at my face after thirty years.

Thank you for putting up with me sobbing over my inability to use technology.

Thank you for solving the tech issues I was sobbing over.

Thank you for suggesting that once I'm published, I can behave like an eccentric writer and people will forgive me.

Thank you.

Index

Interested in applying critical thinking to leadership communication, collaboration and culture?

Connect with Annie:

in linkedin.com/in/annie-mccubbin-coup
© instagram.com/anniemccubbin
f facebook.com/anniemccubbincoup

Annie is the founder and director of COUP, a professional development consultancy.

COUP provides training and executive coaching in communication, collaboration, composure and cognition – or, as this book describes it, critical thinking.

COUP has been serving corporates and profit-for-purpose organisations in Australia and abroad from 2001, and offers a suite of professional development interventions that help leaders and teams cut the drama that gets in the way of progress, focus on what's really happening and lift performance to new levels.

COUP also produces video for internal communication and social media content marketing.

Annie loves a chat, especially when it helps get things back on track.

coup.co

Also by Annie McCubbin

**If you loved *Why Smart Women Make Bad Decisions*,
then grab a copy of the sequel.**

In *Why Smart Women Buy the Lies*, we rejoin Kat, who, after seeing off her narcissistic boyfriend, believes that this is the year her life will click into gear. She is in a relationship with a lovely, decent man, she's enjoying her well-paid job and she has adopted a large groodle. Things are looking up!

Then her boss brings in a smooth-talking business guru, her neighbour employs a psychic to rid her flat of a curse and stylish but mysterious neighbours move in upstairs. Things start to go awry. Her happy life starts to fracture. Her relationship is threatened, the groodle disappears and she gets scammed.

Available from all good bookstores and at majorstreet.com.au

Follow Annie on Instagram: instagram.com/anniemccubbin

major st
PUBLISHING

We hope you enjoy reading this book. We'd love you to post a review on social media or your favourite bookseller site. Please include the hashtag #majorstreetpublishing.

Major Street Publishing specialises in business, leadership, personal finance and motivational non-fiction books. If you'd like to receive regular updates about new Major Street books, email info@majorstreet.com.au and ask to be added to our mailing list.

Visit majorstreet.com.au to find out more about our books and authors.

We'd love you to follow us on social media.

linkedin.com/company/major-street-publishing

facebook.com/MajorStreetPublishing

instagram.com/majorstreetpublishing

@MajorStreetPub